ALFRED PORTALE SIMPLE PLEASURES

ALFRED PORTALE
SIMPLE PLEASURES

HOME COOKING FROM
THE GOTHAM BAR AND GRILL'S
ACCLAIMED CHEF

ALFRED PORTALE
AND ANDREW FRIEDMAN

WILLIAM MORROW
An Imprint of HarperCollinsPublishers

HarperCollins books may be purchased for educational, business, or sales promotional use. For information please write: Special Markets Department, HarperCollins Publishers Inc., 10 East 53rd Street, New York, NY 10022.

FIRST EDITION

Designed by Marysarah Quinn

Photographs by Gozen Koshida

Printed on acid-free paper

Library of Congress Cataloging-in-Publication Data

Portale, Alfred
     [Simple pleasures]
     Alfred Portale simple pleasures : home cooking from the Gotham Bar and Grill's acclaimed chef / Alfred Portale and Andrew Friedman.
          p.   cm.
     Includes index.
     ISBN 0-06-053502-4
     1. Cookery, American.   I. Friedman, Andrew.   II. Gotham Bar and Grill.
III. Title.

   TX715.P8374   2004
   641.5973—dc22

                                   2003071008

04   05   06   07   08 WBC/TP 10   9   8   7   6   5   4   3   2   1

TO MY LOVING MOTHER AND FATHER

CONTENTS

ACKNOWLEDGMENTS

I'D LIKE TO THANK THE FOLLOWING PEOPLE, ALL OF WHOM MADE ESSENTIAL CONTRIBUTIONS TO THIS BOOK:

Harriet Bell, my editor at William Morrow, for her guidance and support throughout the process;

Andrew Friedman, my longtime co-author, for another book well done;

Gozen Koshida, for his keen photographic eye and consistent professionalism, and Raiko Akehi, for her help with the photography sessions;

Helen Chardack, for urging me to do this book and for developing many outstanding recipes, especially the desserts;

Deborah Racicot, Gotham Bar and Grill's pastry chef, for contributing some excellent dessert recipes of her own;

Jacinto Guadarrama, my longtime chef de cuisine, for recipe testing and help during the photo sessions;

Seth Kutzen, for his invaluable assistance in testing the recipes;

Saundra Blackman and Lisa Scott, of Gotham Bar and Grill, for their organizational help;

Devonia—Antiques for Dining; Lalique, North America, Inc.; and Porcelaines Bernardaud;

Viking Range Corporation, for the use of their world-class equipment;

All-Clad, for their exceptional line of cookware and knives;

Magnet Communications' Charly Rok, Gotham Bar and Grill's publicist, for her infectious enthusiasm and tireless work ethic;

My Gotham partners Rick and Robert Rathe, Jeff Bliss, and especially Jerome Kretchmer;

And Gotham's staff and customers, past and present, for a great twenty years and counting.

IN ADDITION TO THE ABOVE, ANDREW FRIEDMAN WOULD LIKE TO THANK:

Lucy Baker, of William Morrow, for all her help;

Ann Limpert, for her research assistance;

And as always, Caitlin Connelly Friedman, for the value she places on life's simple pleasures.

INTRODUCTION

THE PHRASE "SIMPLE PLEASURES" DESCRIBES UNCOMPLICATED but highly enjoyable diversions. Simple pleasures can occur naturally or can be the product of the work of others: listening to a favorite piece of music, walking on the beach, or watching a stunning sunset. Others require some time and effort, but the work itself is part of the pleasure, like spending a warm summer day tending a backyard garden.

To me, "simple pleasures" means the same thing in the kitchen that it does elsewhere: satisfying dishes that are relatively, and often surprisingly, easy to cook. In this book, I'm going to share recipes for my favorite simple pleasures, more than one hundred that anyone can make, regardless of culinary skill, budget, or available time. I hope their simplicity earns them a place in your personal repertoire, to be called on for any occasion, from a solitary lunch, to a weeknight family meal, to a Saturday dinner party.

For the most part, when I cook at home, even if the guests include other chefs, I keep it simple. Some of the most memorable dinner parties I've hosted at home have been centered around grilled pizzas, jerked chicken, or a whole roasted suckling pig. Sometimes I'll offer something elemental, focusing on one perfect ingredient, like the time I secured a few pounds of red Spanish prawns, marinated them in orange zest, garlic, and smoked paprika, grilled them, and set them out for dinner.

This is also what I look for when I go out. When I get together with other chefs after our own kitchens have closed for the night, my preferred destination is likely to be a Thai or Indian restaurant, a trattoria with a great wine list that serves great pastas and wood-oven-baked pizza, or a restaurant that we've heard makes the most authentic barbecue in the city. These foods, as flavorful as they are uncomplicated, are what I crave after a long night in the kitchen and, on a culinary level, appreciate just as much as more ambitious cooking.

Most of the recipes here have been developed in my home kitchen or conceived expressly for this book; the rest are Gotham Bar and Grill dishes that have been simplified to make them as accessible and user-friendly as possible. They illustrate how much harmonious flavor can be produced by using just a few carefully selected and prepared ingredients. You'll find that the ingredients lists are relatively short and that most of the items called for are available in supermarkets. There are no luxury items like caviar, foie gras, lobster, or truffles, although a few are suggested as optional additions. And the recipe steps themselves are fairly easy; you don't need to have an expert's deft hands to follow them. I hope that, taken together, these recipes help dispel the notion that you have to spend hour upon hour in the kitchen in order to make great food.

It's been said that simplicity is the key to perfection, and there's a very good reason for that: when something is simple, each element carries a lot of responsibility for the overall success of the whole. In some ways, creating simple recipes requires the same effort as creating more complex ones, because you have to make more of an impact with fewer ingredients. For the home cook, this means seeking out the best quality you can find, because each item will likely make more of an impact than it would in a more elaborate recipe. Once you've found those ingredients, it means learning to coax out as much flavor as possible through seasoning and cooking. Where appropriate, this book offers guidance on each stage of the process, with tips on selecting ingredients and cooking them properly.

In my first book, and to some extent in my second, I showed home cooks how to be home chefs, by presenting main courses that comprised three or more components: a fish, poultry, or meat, along with the appropriate sauce and side dishes. In this book, I've adopted the opposite tack: components are presented separately, often with pairing suggestions, so you can build as much of a meal as you'd like.

You'll notice that a few themes emerge—some recurring strategies for realizing these simple pleasures. They are:

THE ELEMENT OF SURPRISE

One of the greatest tactical advantages for a cook is the element of surprise. Springing something unexpected on your friends and family can elevate a simple meal to something quite special.

For example, serve dinner-party guests a grilled steak with creamed spinach on the side and they can't help but be underwhelmed. Worse, they will no doubt compare those components to other versions they've tasted over the years. But if you present a different take on them, perhaps serving Filet Mignon with Madeira Sauce (page 178) and pairing it with Creamed Spinach Custards with Extra Virgin Olive Oil and Parmesan Cheese (page 197), then you'll be offering something original, though reassuringly familiar, that can be enjoyed on its own terms.

Surprise can also be generated by juxtaposition, pairing ingredients or flavors that haven't traditionally been presented together—for example, expanding a classic French onion soup by making it with gratinéed pumpkin and sage, or even something as simple as adding curry powder to creamed corn. And there's perhaps no surprise diners enjoy more than a tried and true recipe put to a new use. I've done quite a bit of that here as well, turning a classic soup into a sauce or applying the flavors traditionally associated with one dish to another.

SUMS GREATER THAN THEIR PARTS

You might be surprised to see how short many of the ingredients lists are. In order to maintain a certain degree of simplicity, I've kept recipes down to their bare essentials, using all the tools in a cook's arsenal to maximize each of the ingredients.

For example, I employ compound butters, create pan sauces, and steam a sauce into existence along with the shellfish in the pot.

INTERNATIONAL INGREDIENTS

While I didn't set out to write a multicultural book, these pages also feature ingredients and recipes from places as diverse as China, France, Italy, Morocco, and Spain—those simple pleasures I've enjoyed at the restaurants I like to visit with fellow chefs. I include a number of dishes that are everyday food in their home countries, but served here, they are pleasantly surprising. The cooking remains fairly uncomplicated, but the ingredients seem exciting and exotic.

With this in mind, perhaps the most important resource this book draws on is the modern pantry. Just a decade ago, many of these ingredients would have been unavailable to the average American home cook, especially outside of a big city. But today chipotle peppers, five-spice powder, pancetta, and many other specialty foods are available in gourmet shops and most supermarkets.

The Modern Pantry (pages 11–17) describes the ingredients used throughout this book, telling you a bit about their origin, their most common uses, and where to look for them in your supermarket.

I had a great time developing the recipes in this book. Many of them have become household favorites. Others have been dressed up and added to the menu at Gotham Bar and Grill. I present all of them to you with the highest recommendation I know: I enjoy cooking and eating them myself.

HOW TO USE THIS BOOK

THIS BOOK IS DIVIDED INTO CHAPTERS THAT ARE FAIRLY self-explanatory: Salads, Starters, and Small Plates; Soups, Sandwiches, and Pizzas; Pasta and Risotto; Main Courses; Accompaniments and Side Dishes; and Desserts. It should be noted, however, that several of the recipes might be used in ways beyond what these chapter titles indicate. There are salads that can be called on as a main course or side dish; pizzas that can be served as a starter; and soups that can be a meal in themselves.

Following many recipes, you will find a Pairing note that offers a suggestion or two for matching the recipe with others in the book. This feature also sometimes mentions good first-course/main-course combinations, drawing from other chapters with an eye toward complementary flavors and economies of time and money. In the case of desserts, I recommend savory dishes that might precede them.

Also included are two popular features from my previous books:

VARIATIONS

This is where you'll find substitution suggestions for everything from seasonal ingredients to options for accommodating personal taste. For example, in the Fingerling Potato Salad with Mussels, Fennel, and Saffron (page 50), I suggest that fennel-lovers replace the white wine with Pernod to punch up the anise flavor. And in the recipe for the Fig, Prosciutto, and Arugula Salad with a Balsamic-Honey Drizzle (page 43), I explain why you might replace the figs with sliced Anjou pear, or substitute Spanish Manchego for the goat cheese. This is also where I give instructions for alternative cooking methods, such as pan-roasting the meat in the Grilled Marinated Pork Chops (page 176) if grilling isn't an option.

Here I offer ways to augment a dish by adding ingredients or by finishing it with anything from extravagant additions like caviar to more everyday possibilities like infused oils and compound butters. For example, a teaspoon of grated ginger added along with the saffron brings a lively flavor to the Carrot-Saffron Soup with Crème Fraîche (page 71). Finish the soup by stirring in some grated orange zest and drizzling the surface with orange oil. Or add roasted root vegetables to Pan-Roasted Squab with Butter-Braised Savoy Cabbage and Green Apples (page 172) to turn it into a more complete meal. Flavor building can also be as simple and effective as topping Pappardelle with Braised Lamb Shank and Fontina (page 117) with a dollop of ricotta cheese to provide a cool, creamy counterpoint to the sauce.

Less familiar ingredients, such as farro, grapeseed oil, and *ras el hanut,* are described in The Modern Pantry. This is followed by Modern Equipment, where I point you toward a few tools that I find indispensable in the kitchen.

THE MODERN PANTRY

ANCHOVIES

Salt-cured anchovies, sold flat or coiled in small tins or jars, are a flavoring agent for salad dressings, the most famous example being Caesar dressing, and also a canny way to boost other flavors in sauces. They are easy to find in your supermarket, and once opened, they can be stored in their container in the refrigerator for up to 2 months, provided they are covered with oil and the container is well sealed. I usually purchase jarred anchovies because it's easy to reseal and store them. If you buy yours in a tin, transfer the unused anchovies to a jar and top them with oil before refrigerating.

BALSAMIC VINEGAR

It surprises many people to learn that balsamic vinegar, with its tawny, portlike tint, is fashioned from the juice of white Trebbiano grapes. The juice darkens as it ages in barrels, turning intensely sweet. The best manufacturers move the juice from one barrel to another over a period of several years, subjecting it to the distinct effects of different woods. Balsamic vinegar was first produced in Modena, Italy, which is still widely regarded as the only producer of "real" balsamic; look for the designation "aceto balsamico tradizionale di Modena" on the label. Conversely, be wary of other balsamic vinegars, many of which are cooked and artificially flavored to produce imitation balsamic.

CANNED TOMATOES

Without question, the best canned tomatoes are San Marzano tomatoes, which—contrary to popular belief—isn't a brand; it's a town at the base of Italy's Mount Vesuvius, where soil and climate conditions produce superior tomatoes. San Marzano tomatoes are sweet plum tomatoes; they are available whole or crushed. If you can't find them, look for Muir Glen, an organic brand produced in the United States.

CAPERS

Capers are the flower buds of a Mediterranean bush that are picked and sun-dried. Most often used as a last-minute addition to fish sauces, they range in size from tiny to huge Italian capers. They can be packed in brine or salt; either should be rinsed and drained before using.

CHIPOTLE PEPPERS

Chipotle peppers are smoked jalapeño peppers (see page 14) that are sold canned in a spicy tomato-based adobo sauce. Many recipes, including one in this book, call for the chipotle to be pureed together with the adobo.

CRÈME FRAÎCHE

Crème fraîche is cream that's been aged to the point where it begins to thicken—at least that's how it's produced in its native France, where the bacteria that forms in the unpasteurized cream does the work. Here in the U. S., where cream must, by law, be pasteurized, buttermilk or sour cream is added to produce the desired effect. Crème fraîche is something of a culinary dual citizen, as suitable for bringing a velvety richness to soups and sauces (where it doesn't curdle when cooked, like regular cream) as it is for topping off a dessert. Some markets carry crème fraîche in the dairy refrigerator; those with a serious cheese department might store it there.

EXTRA VIRGIN OLIVE OIL

Produced by a cold pressing, extra virgin olive oil is the best, most full-flavored, and fruitiest of all olive oil. Each producer's extra virgin olive oil is distinct, with flavors that run the gamut from mild to peppery and colors that range from strawlike yellow to pale green. It's also important to know that not all extra virgin olive oils are created equal; the best generally come from Italy, Spain, Greece, and France, and you should expect to pay more as you move up the strata of quality. Use extra virgin olive oil as a condiment for finishing dishes rather than as a cooking medium.

FARRO (SPELT)

The Italian farro (spelt to Americans) is a nutty-flavored grain that's often used like rice. A *farrotto,* for example, is a risotto-like dish made with this grain. Farro can be cooked and added to soups and stews, or cooled and used as the basis for salads. Look for it in specialty and health food stores.

FIVE-SPICE POWDER

Generally available in the spice section of a supermarket, this popular Chinese blend comprises equal parts of ground cinnamon, cloves, fennel seed, star anise, and Szechuan peppercorns.

FLEUR DE SEL

Fleur de sel comes from the same marshes in the south of Brittany as sea salt but is in a class by itself. Think of it as a condiment rather than a seasoning; it's best used to finish a dish. Put another way, it's what balsamic vinegar is to regular vinegar and extra virgin olive oil is to regular olive oil. Its high cost is understandable when you consider the labor-intensive manner in which it's produced: Fleur de sel crystals gather in a film on the edges of the marshes or float on the surface of the water as it evaporates. These crystals are carefully skimmed off and allowed to sun-dry and whiten in the open air. You may not find fleur de sel next to the other salts in your supermarket; look for it in specialty and gourmet shops.

GRAPESEED OIL

This neutral-flavored oil—made by pressing the seeds of grapes, gathered after the fruit has been pressed for wine—has a high smoking point, which makes it a good choice for sautéing. It's also a superb selection for dressings and vinaigrettes where you don't want to taste the oil. It wasn't that long ago that it was difficult to find grapeseed oil in the United States, but its popularity among chefs has increased its profile and availability.

HARISSA

Available in jars and tubes at Middle Eastern markets and many gourmet shops, this spicy Tunisian condiment is made from hot peppers and tomatoes. It's added to a wide range of dishes, including couscous and pastas.

ISRAELI COUSCOUS

Israeli couscous isn't actually a grain, but rather a pea-size bit of semolina pasta that's used like a grain as the basis of salads and pasta dishes and as an addition to soups. (Traditional couscous is also a pasta fashioned from hard-wheat semolina, but its smaller size makes it look more like an actual grain.)

JALAPEÑO PEPPERS

The jalapeño is perhaps the best-known and most readily available spicy chile pepper in the United States, but it's by no means the hottest, especially if you remove its seeds. I appreciate it for its great flavor, which is often overlooked. It's usually recommended that one wear latex gloves when working with chile peppers, but this isn't essential if you're careful to wash your hands, knife, and cutting board after using them, so the oil isn't transferred to your skin. For this reason, I slice these peppers last when preparing ingredients.

LEMON OLIVE OIL

Italians produce lemon olive oil by crushing lemons and olives together, producing a bright, citrus-accented extra virgin olive oil in which both flavors are present. Available at specialty shops and gourmet stores, lemon olive oil makes an impact when drizzled over fish and certain soups and salads.

OLIVES

A wide selection of Mediterranean olives are available to American home cooks today, and I recommend them to you for a simple hors d'oeuvre or as a flavoring in countless dishes. Many gourmet markets and supermarkets now have olive bars. Green olives are harvested when they are fully grown but not ripe; black olives are fully ripened. Olives are preserved by either fermentation or brine-curing, which grants them a long shelf life; other flavors, such as lemon, herbs, or pepper, are often added. Each olive has its own distinct texture and flavor. Some of my favorite varieties are Gaeta, Niçoise, Picholine, Moroccan, and Sicilian.

PANCETTA

Pancetta is commonly referred to as Italian bacon, but this is something of a misnomer. Yes, it does come from the belly of the pig, like American bacon, but unlike American bacon, it's not smoked. Rather, pancetta is cured in a combination of salt and spices that imparts a complex flavor. Pancetta is often used to begin a recipe; the fat it renders is used in place of butter or oil, carrying the flavors throughout the dish. For this use, purchase ¼-inch-thick slices and dice them. If you buy more than you need, pancetta freezes well.

PASTA
I use both fresh and dried pasta, although I never use fresh pasta shapes, like penne or ziti. Imported dried Italian pastas are available in most supermarkets and I urge you to use those brands, which tend to have a superior mouthfeel and flavor. High-quality fresh pasta can often be found at gourmet markets and Italian specialty shops. In a pinch, mass-produced supermarket brands can be used, but take extra care not to overcook them.

PRESERVED LEMONS
Preserved lemons are whole lemons that have been stored in brine for anywhere from several weeks to several months. During this time, the salt (and other flavor enhancers, such as cinnamon, cloves, and coriander) penetrates the peel and the flesh, softening them. In Morocco and other North African countries, these lemons are served with fish, poultry, and meat. Preserved lemons are easily made at home (see recipe below) and are available in jars at gourmet stores.

5 lemons, quartered lengthwise
1 cinnamon stick, broken
3 bay leaves
⅓ cup salt
1⅓ cups freshly squeezed lemon juice

Arrange the lemon quarters in layers in a 1-quart jar, topping each layer with some of the cinnamon, bay leaves, and salt. Pour the lemon juice over the lemon quarters. Seal the jar with a tight-fitting lid. Set in a cool, dry place for about 1 month.

PRESERVED TUNA
Imported preserved tuna and canned American tuna have very little in common. Preserved tuna is the very best canned or jarred tuna, submerged in high-quality extra virgin olive oil, and usually produced in Italy or Spain. It's more expensive than the usual canned tuna, but worth it. There's a recipe for making your own on page 60.

PROSCIUTTO DI PARMA
Prosciutto is ham that has been seasoned, salt-cured, and air-dried. The best comes from the Parma region of Italy. It should be rosy pink, not excessively dry or salty.

RAS EL HANUT
This Moroccan spice blend contains up to fifty ingredients, including anise, cardamom, cinnamon, cloves, ginger, mace, nutmeg, peppercorns,

dried rose, and turmeric. It's used to enhance soups and stews that are served with couscous. The name, by the way, means "head of shop," a reference to the fact that each shop owner makes his own blend. It's sometimes spelled *ras el hanout*.

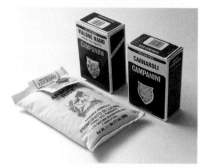

RICE

Arborio, Canaroli, and Vialone Nano are three varieties of Italian rice used for making risotto; their ability to absorb a lot of liquid and their high starch content are crucial. (The starch released as the rice is cooked is what binds risotto together.) These rice varieties have the shortest and fattest grains, giving risotto a nice plump texture. Arborio, from the Piedmont region of Italy, is better known here, but look for Vialone Nano and Canaroli; both have a smaller grain that yields an even creamier result.

SAFFRON

A key ingredient in the classic dishes of many countries, like Spain's paella, France's bouillabaise, and Italy's risotto Milanese, saffron is what that gives those dishes their distinct golden-yellow tint, as it does in a carrot-saffron soup and a few mussel dishes in this book. Don't buy powdered saffron. Purchase the natural threads. Yes, saffron is expensive, but no recipe calls for more than a pinch or two, so it lasts a long time. Many markets now sell small packets of saffron, often found at the register.

SESAME OIL

Yes, sesame oil is actually made from sesame seeds. Its available in light and dark forms. Store it in a cool, dark place and use it as quickly as possible; it loses its impact after six to eight months.

SHERRY VINEGAR

This full-bodied vinegar is produced only in Jerez, the brandy capital of Spain, where it is made from Palomino Fino grapes. It is aged over a period of approximately six years, during which time it develops a complex flavor and a beautiful pale color. Sherry vinegar can be found in the same section of your supermarket as other vinegars.

SMOKED PAPRIKA (*PIMENTÓN DE LA VERA*)

Available in specialty markets, smoked paprika is made from capsicum peppers that are hand-harvested each October, then smoked over a smoldering oak fire for fifteen days, during which time they soak up the wood flavor while maintaining their distinct red tint. They are then stone-ground into a potent powder that's far more complex in flavor than traditional paprika.

SOY SAUCE

The best supermarket brands of soy sauce are identified as whole-bean or organic, which are generally indications of relatively high quality. The Japanese are fanatical about soy sauce and produce a wide range of super-premium brands, many of which are shepherded by centuries'-old family firms and are so rarified that they're comparable to wines, made in small batches and available to a fortunate few. You won't find the very best of these in the United States, but you can find premium brands in Japanese markets and specialty stores.

TRUFFLE OIL

If you love the intense flavor and aromatic quality of white or black truffles, a less expensive way to have them at your disposal is white or black truffle oil. These oils are made by infusing a high-quality olive oil with truffles. Truffle oil can sometimes be found in supermarkets near the olive oils, or perhaps in the Italian specialties section. Because it's so potently flavored, it should be used sparingly.

WALNUT OIL

Made from the meat of walnuts, walnut oil is a useful, concentrated way to add walnut flavor to dressings or as a final embellishment to soup. Look for French walnut oil. Refrigerate it or keep it in a cool, dark place after opening; it has a limited shelf life and its flavor will diminish after about six months.

MODERN EQUIPMENT

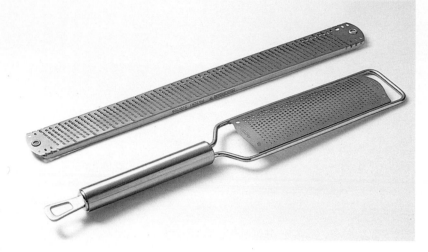

MICROPLANE GRATER ZESTER

The key difference between a box grater and a microplane zester, other than size and shape, is that the latter has hundreds of almost microscopic blades, rather than a few clumsy, jagged holes. (It originated as a woodworking tool; hence the use of the word "plane" in its name.) This instrument is the perfect way to get delicate gratings from citrus fruits, hard cheeses, and nutmeg, to name just a few uses. It can be purchased at any cooking equipment store or on-line site.

EUROPEAN-STYLE PEELER

This inexpensive, lightweight peeler doesn't look significantly different from a swivel-bladed vegetable peeler, but it offers much better control and speed, especially since it doesn't clog as you work. They are usually made in Switzerland; the best-known brand is Kuhn Rikon.

IMMERSION BLENDER

Also known as a hand-blender, this tool consists of a long wand with a rotating blade at the bottom, and it turns every pot into a blender. The immersion blender is found in just about every professional kitchen in the United States. It allows you to puree soups and sauces by moving the instrument in a stirring motion, giving you better control than you get with a standard blender—and involving less cleanup. Kitchenware shops carry them.

JAPANESE MANDOLINE

The mandoline is a stainless steel kitchen tool that makes fine hand-slicing easy. The traditional French mandoline is heavy and can be very expensive. The Japanese make a lightweight version with a plastic frame that is considerably less expensive and does a great job of slic-

ing; it can even julienne. I also use a mandoline to shave hard cheeses. You can find them in Asian markets and housewares stores.

SPICE GRINDER

Just as freshly grinding black pepper is the best way to unleash its full potential, lightly toasting and grinding whole spices as you use them is the optimal way to make the most of their flavor. A coffee grinder is the ideal tool for this task. (Buy a second one just for spices—don't use the one you use to grind coffee beans.)

KNIVES

I could write a whole chapter on knives. Suffice it to say that you should invest in a few high-quality, forged steel knives, preferably manufactured in Germany or Japan. Learn to take care of them and keep them sharp, with either a steel or a stone sharpener.

SALADS, STARTERS, AND SMALL PLATES

THE DISHES IN THIS CHAPTER are grouped together because they all offer something valuable to home cooks: flexibility. They can be served as first courses, as part of a family-style dinner, or as a small meal in their own right.

There's no lack of precedent for versatile small plates that can play different roles on different days. Many cultures have a generations-old tradition of eating this way, from Spanish tapas to Venetian cicchetti to Middle Eastern meze. In recent years, small plates have caught on throughout the United States, as is seen in the increasing number of restaurants that offer tasting menus comprising five, six, or more courses, each of them a small plate.

Many of the recipes that follow can be served in the same freestyle manner, and I encourage you to do just that, especially if you are serving a large group of people—it's fun to pass the dishes around, comparing notes and declaring favorites.

Small plates allow for creativity and variety, because each recipe is an end in itself; each little composition stands on its own. Pull a number of them together and it's quite possible that you'll have something more memorable than a traditionally organized meal. The flexibility of thinking this way opens up many doors. Portobello Mushroom Salad with Green Lentils, White Runner Beans, and Tarragon, for example, can be served on its own as a starter, passed along with other small dishes in a one-course meal, or paired with grilled or roasted birds or meat as an accompaniment.

Many of these dishes can serve as a small meal or main course. The Spicy Shrimp Salad with Mango, Avocado, and Lime Vinaigrette and the Honey-Ginger Glazed Quail on Wilted Lettuces are two examples.

For all the modern motivation in this chapter, there are also a handful of salads that fill their traditional role as a first course, thanks largely to the presence of a leafy green, such as the Fig, Prosciutto, and Arugula Salad and the Frisée Salad with Smoked Bacon, Shiitakes, and Aged Goat Cheese. Each of these can be served as the first course in a classically organized meal, or with a combination of other small plates in a meal customized to suit your own inclination.

BEET SALAD WITH FETA, ORANGE, AND MINT

This simple, vibrant salad extracts everything beets have to offer by first roasting them to concentrate their flavor, then tossing them with orange segments, imbuing the oranges with a crimson tint reminiscent of blood oranges. If you think of feta cheese as dry, crumbly, and excessively salty, you've probably had the ubiquitous, mass-produced Greek variety that's sold in supermarkets. Seek out a high-quality Greek or French feta, with moderate salinity and more creaminess. SERVES 4

2 large beets, washed but not peeled

2 tablespoons olive oil

Coarse salt

Freshly ground black pepper

1 teaspoon freshly squeezed orange juice

2 teaspoons balsamic vinegar

4½ teaspoons extra virgin olive oil

3 oranges, peeled and separated into segments

¼ cup coarsely chopped mint leaves

3 teaspoons minced shallots

About 4 ounces French or Greek feta cheese, crumbled into large pieces (1 cup crumbled)

Preheat the oven to 400°F.

In a bowl, toss the beets with the olive oil and season them with salt and pepper. Put the beets on a roasting pan and cover them with foil. Roast in the preheated oven until tender, about 1½ hours. (They are done when a sharp, thin-bladed knife can easily pierce through to their center.) Remove the pan from the oven, remove the beets from the pan, and set them aside to cool.

While the beets are roasting, make the vinaigrette: In a small bowl, whisk together the orange juice, balsamic vinegar, and extra virgin olive oil. Season to taste with salt and pepper. Set aside.

When they are cool enough to handle, peel the beets and cut them into ½-inch dice. Put them in a bowl with 1 cup of the orange segments, the mint, and the shallots. Add the vinaigrette, season with salt and pepper, and toss gently.

Transfer the salad to a platter. Arrange the cheese and the remaining orange sections on top, and serve.

VARIATIONS

Using minneolas or tangerines in place of the oranges will maintain the character of the salad while varying the degree of sweetness. If you can find them, substitute blood oranges.

No high-quality feta available? Replace it with goat cheese Roquefort, or another blue cheese.

SHAVED FENNEL, GREEN APPLE, AND PECORINO ROMANO SALAD

I grew up in an Italian household in upstate New York, where my mother served simple salads that involved little more than fresh raw vegetables—anything from cauliflower to fennel—tossed with olive oil and seasoned with salt and pepper. Here I've built on that foundation by adding green apple, lemon zest, and parsley. High-quality extra virgin olive oil is key to this salad's success. SERVES 4

2 medium fennel bulbs

2 Granny Smith apples, unpeeled, halved, cored, and thinly sliced

About 1½ ounces pecorino Romano, shaved with a vegetable peeler (½ cup shavings)

1 tablespoon grated lemon zest

¼ cup extra virgin olive oil, plus more for serving

2 tablespoons chopped flat-leaf parsley

Coarse salt

Freshly ground black pepper

Chop off the fronds where they meet the body of one fennel bulb. Halve the fennel, then thinly slice it, using a mandoline or a very sharp, thin-bladed chef's knife. Repeat with the other bulb. You should have 2 cups of slices. Set them aside. Chop 1 tablespoon of the fronds and set it aside separately. Discard the remaining fronds.

Put the fennel and apple slices in a bowl. Add the pecorino Romano, lemon zest, ¼ cup olive oil, and parsley. Toss gently. Taste, and season with salt and pepper.

Arrange the salad on a large, chilled serving plate. Drizzle more olive oil generously over the top, and scatter with the chopped fennel fronds just before serving.

PAIRINGS

Pappardelle with Braised Lamb Shank and Fontina (page 117), perhaps followed by Chocolate-Hazelnut Tiramisù (page 250) for dessert

VARIATIONS

If you can't find pecorino Romano cheese, or simply prefer Parmigiano-Reggiano, by all means substitute it.

Crisp, sweet pears, such as Bosc, are a good autumnal replacement for the apples.

PORTOBELLO MUSHROOM SALAD WITH GREEN LENTILS, WHITE RUNNER BEANS, AND TARRAGON

White beans boast a dual nature; they have the unique ability to take on other flavors while maintaining their own. So cooking white beans in stock rather than water imbues them with a pleasing complexity. This pays big dividends with creamy beans like white runners, the ones used in this dish. Pairing them with lentilles du Puy and tarragon—an often overlooked herb—elevates this salad. SERVES 4

1 cup dried white runner beans or Great Northern beans

Coarse salt

⅓ cup dried French lentils, preferably the French ones known as lentilles du Puy

1½ cups Chicken Stock (recipe follows)

Freshly ground black pepper

3 small portobello mushrooms, stems discarded

½ cup plus 1 tablespoon extra virgin olive oil

1 tablespoon minced shallot

1 tablespoon plus 1 teaspoon sherry vinegar

1 tablespoon chopped tarragon

Soak the beans overnight in enough cold water to cover them by 1 inch (see Note). Drain.

Bring a saucepan of salted water to a boil. Add the lentils and cook them until tender, about 25 minutes. Drain the lentils and spread them out on a cookie sheet to cool them as quickly as possible.

Pour the stock and 1 cup of water into a pot. Bring the liquid to a boil, add the runner beans, and cook them until tender, about 50 minutes. Remove the pot from the heat, season the cooking liquid with salt and pepper, and let the beans cool in the liquid. Drain.

Preheat the oven to 450°F.

Place the mushrooms in a baking pan, and drizzle them on both sides with the 1 tablespoon olive oil. Season them with salt and pepper. Roast the mushrooms in the preheated oven for 12 minutes. Turn them over and roast until tender, about another 3 minutes. Remove the pan from the oven, let the mushrooms cool, and then cut them into ¼-inch-thick slices.

In a salad bowl, toss together the beans, shallot, lentils, and mushrooms.

In a small bowl, whisk together the remaining ½ cup olive oil, the sherry vinegar, and the tarragon, and season with salt and pepper. Drizzle this dressing over the salad. Toss, taste, and adjust the acidity if necessary by adding a few more drops of sherry vinegar.

Serve family-style from the center of the table.

Note: If you prefer, use this quick-soak method for the beans:

1. Put the beans in a large pot and add cold water to cover by about 3 inches.

2. Bring the water to a rapid simmer over medium-high heat. Adjust the heat so the beans simmer vigorously for 2 minutes. Do not let the simmer turn into a full boil.

3. Remove the pot from the heat, cover, and let the beans cool in the liquid for at least 1 hour. Drain.

VARIATION
While they won't have the same earthy quality, shiitakes can stand in for the portobellos.

FLAVOR BUILDING
Add goat cheese and/or ½ cup chopped lightly toasted walnuts.

CHICKEN STOCK

MAKES ABOUT 2½ QUARTS

6 pounds chicken bones, coarsely chopped (substitute wings if bones or carcasses are unavailable)

1 large onion, peeled and chopped

1 small carrot, peeled and coarsely chopped

1 small celery stalk, coarsely chopped

1 whole garlic head, halved crosswise

2 thyme sprigs

2 flat-leaf parsley sprigs

1 teaspoon whole black peppercorns

1 bay leaf

Put the chicken in a large stockpot and add cold water to cover by 2 inches. Bring to a boil over medium-high heat, skimming off any foam that rises to the surface. Add all the remaining ingredients. Reduce the heat to low and simmer gently, uncovered, for at least 6 hours or overnight.

Strain the stock into a large bowl, and let in cool completely. Skim off and discard the clear yellow fat that rises to the surface. Or refrigerate the stock until the fat solidifies, approximately 4 hours, then scrape it off with a spoon.

The stock can be refrigerated for up to 3 days or frozen for up to 2 months.

WHITE BEAN CROSTINI WITH WHITE TRUFFLE OIL

The proper use of the words *bruschetta* and *crostini* baffles even the most passionate lovers of Italian food. As near as I can figure it, bruschetta and crostini are the same thing—a slice of grilled or toasted bread topped with meat, vegetables, or both. To most people in the United States, "bruschetta" connotes a tomato, garlic, and basil topping while "crostini" suggests sautéed chicken livers, but those are not the actual definitions.

These crostini are topped with white beans. Simmering the beans in a flavorful stock with six whole garlic cloves imparts powerful flavor. A drizzle of truffle oil finishes this hors d'oeuvre with an alluring fragrance. SERVES 6

1 quart Chicken Stock (page 31)

1 cup dried Great Northern beans, soaked overnight in cold water to cover

6 garlic cloves, peeled

1 bay leaf

Coarse salt

Freshly ground white pepper

3 tablespoons extra virgin olive oil

1 bunch scallions, white and light green parts, thinly sliced crosswise (about 1/3 cup sliced)

1 tablespoon chopped flat-leaf parsley

White truffle oil, for drizzling

1 baguette, cut crosswise into 1/3-inch-thick slices and lightly toasted

Pour the chicken stock into a pot set over medium-high heat. Add the beans, garlic, and bay leaf, bring to a simmer, and let simmer for 50 minutes. Season with salt and pepper. Let the beans cool in the liquid; then drain the beans, reserving the liquid. Discard the bay leaf. Separate out and reserve the garlic cloves.

Put the beans in a bowl and coarsely crush them (a potato masher works well for this). Mash in 2 or 3 of the garlic cloves, or more to taste, and stir. Work in the olive oil with a wooden spoon, taking care to keep the mixture fairly coarse. If the mixture seems too thick, work in some of the reserved cooking liquid. Season with salt and pepper. Stir in the scallions, parsley, and, if desired, more garlic.

Spoon the mixture into a serving bowl, and drizzle with white truffle oil. Serve from the bowl with a basket of the crisp toasts and a bottle of truffle oil so people can add more to taste.

VARIATIONS

In place of the white truffle oil, use black truffle oil, a nut oil, or more extra virgin olive oil.

MUSHROOM CROSTINI WITH THYME AND TRUFFLE OIL

I learned to make this creamy, potentially addictive mushroom condiment from French chef Michel Guérard. Cooking the mushrooms in a small amount of water is essential to getting the flavor just right. The lemon juice isn't added for its taste so much as it is for the fact that its acidity keeps the mushrooms attractively white. MAKES 1 CUP

8 ounces button mushrooms, stems removed, thinly sliced

1 small shallot, peeled and minced

1½ teaspoons freshly squeezed lemon juice

1 garlic clove, peeled and thinly sliced

1 thyme sprig

Coarse salt

Freshly ground white pepper

½ cup extra virgin olive oil

About 3 tablespoons white truffle oil

1 baguette, cut crosswise into ⅓-inch-thick slices and lightly toasted

Put the mushrooms in a saucepan and add just enough water to come level with the top of the mushrooms. Add the shallot, lemon juice, garlic, and thyme, and season with salt and pepper. Cover and bring to a simmer over medium heat. Continue to simmer until the mushrooms are tender, 4 to 5 minutes.

Remove the pan from the heat and let the mushrooms cool in the liquid; then strain them, reserving the liquid. Put the solids in the bowl of a blender. With the motor running, add the olive oil in a thin, steady stream. Then add the truffle oil, to taste, in the same manner. (For a less intensely flavored puree, substitute some of the reserved cooking liquid for the truffle oil.) Scrape the mixture out into a bowl, and season to taste with salt and pepper.

The puree can be covered and refrigerated for up to 24 hours. Let it come to room temperature before serving or using.

Spoon the puree into a serving bowl, and serve from the bowl with a basket of the crisp toasts.

VARIATIONS

Substitute hazelnut oil for the truffle oil.

Use this puree as a dip for vegetables, or as an unexpected pizza topping (page 98).

ENDIVE SALAD WITH TANGERINES, GOLDEN BEETS, AND HAZELNUT VINAIGRETTE

Beets can sometimes overpower other ingredients in a recipe, either with their potent, sweet flavor or by staining everything red. By using golden beets, which have a more mellow flavor and don't "bleed out," this salad keeps each of its components distinct. SERVES 4

1 bunch (about 8) baby yellow or candy-cane beets (3 medium beets can be substituted)

1 tablespoon extra virgin olive oil

Coarse salt

Freshly ground black pepper

3 large Belgian endives, cores removed, leaves cut into 2-inch-thick slices

2 cups (approximately 1 bunch) watercress, thick stems removed

3 tablespoons shallots, peeled and finely chopped

3 tablespoons hazelnut oil

1 tablespoon plus 1 teaspoon sherry vinegar

3 tangerines, peeled and sectioned

¼ cup hazelnuts, toasted, skins rubbed off with a clean kitchen towel, coarsely chopped

Put the beets in a large pot. Cover with cold water and lightly salt the water. Set the pot over high heat and bring the water to a boil. Continue to boil until a sharp, thin-bladed knife pierces easily into the beets' center, 15 to 20 minutes. Drain the beets and let cool.

Peel the beets and slice them crosswise into ¼-inch-thick rounds. Put them in a salad bowl, add the endive, watercress, and shallots, and toss.

Pour the hazelnut oil into a separate bowl, add the vinegar, and whisk together. Pour the dressing over the salad, season with salt and pepper, and toss. Scatter the tangerines and hazelnuts over the salad and serve family-style from the center of the table.

VARIATIONS

If you do not have any hazelnut oil, substitute walnut oil or extra virgin olive oil. If opting for walnut oil, select a French brand, which is of the highest quality.

FLAVOR BUILDING

Crumble a few ounces of feta, goat, or blue cheese over the salad just before serving.

STEAMED LEEKS AND RED POTATOES WITH FRESH TOMATO VINAIGRETTE

This dish brings together two versatile techniques that you will find multiple applications for. First is the one for cooking the leeks—seasoning them with olive oil and salt *before* steaming, so they take on a rich flavor as they cook. Second is the vinaigrette, a perfect one for showing off gorgeous late-summer tomatoes. It's ideal for dressing other vegetables and also as a warm vinaigrette for grilled fish. SERVES 6

4 large leeks

Coarse salt

4 tablespoons extra virgin olive oil

2 medium red potatoes

2 medium ripe tomatoes

½ medium red onion, peeled and chopped

3 garlic cloves, peeled and finely chopped

1 tablespoon capers, rinsed and chopped

1 teaspoon chopped anchovy fillet

1 tablespoon coarsely chopped pitted Niçoise olives

2 teaspoons red wine vinegar

Freshly ground black pepper

4 or 5 large basil leaves, cut into a chiffonade

Discard the dark green tops of the leeks. Slice the leeks on a sharp diagonal into ½-inch-thick pieces. Separate the rings into a colander (or the insert of a vegetable steamer) and rinse under cold water. Season with salt and 1 tablespoon of the olive oil. Bring an inch or two of water to a boil in a large saucepan. Put the colander over the pan, cover, and steam until the leeks are just tender, approximately 5 minutes. Transfer the leeks to a bowl to cool.

Repeat this process with the potatoes: Cut them (unpeeled) into ½-inch-thick rounds, put them in the colander, and season with salt and 1 tablespoon of the olive oil. Steam, covered, until just cooked through, approximately 6 minutes. Transfer them to a plate to cool.

Bring a large pot of water to a boil. Fill a large bowl halfway with ice water.

Prepare the tomatoes by cutting a shallow X on the end of each one. Carve out the stem and a bit of the flesh around it. Submerge the tomatoes in the boiling water for 20 seconds; then transfer them to the ice-water bath to stop the cooking. Transfer them to a bowl to cool completely. Once the tomatoes have cooled, peel, seed, and cut them into large dice.

Over medium heat, heat 1 tablespoon of the olive oil in a sauté pan. Add the onions, garlic, capers, anchovies, and olives. Quickly sauté. After 1 minute, add the tomatoes and sauté briefly to heat through, just a minute or two. Transfer the mixture to a bowl and gently stir in the red wine vinegar and the remaining 1 tablespoon

olive oil. Let cool to room temperature. Season to taste with salt and pepper.

Compose the dish by arranging the potatoes around the edge of a serving platter. Put the leeks in the center. Spoon some of the fresh tomato vinaigrette over the vegetables, and garnish with the basil. Pass the extra vinaigrette alongside.

PAIRING

Preserved Tuna with Potatoes, Arugula, and Scallions
(page 59)

VARIATION

Steaming sliced sweet Vidalia onions in place of the leeks will yield a similar result.

FLAVOR BUILDING

Blue cheese has great affinity with leeks and tomatoes. Crumbling some over the salad is a fine way to appreciate the combination.

ISRAELI COUSCOUS SALAD
WITH GRILLED SUMMER VEGETABLES

This colorful salad features vibrant summer vegetables that are grilled, chopped, and then tossed with Israeli couscous. Unlike its Moroccan namesake, whose grains are smaller, lighter, and fluffier, Israeli couscous is pea-sized. It's equally at home in soups, as the central ingredient in a pasta dish, or tossed, with vegetables as it is here, to create a substantial salad. SERVES 4

1 medium zucchini, halved lengthwise

1 medium yellow squash, halved lengthwise

1 Japanese eggplant, halved lengthwise

1 medium red onion, peeled, halved, and sliced into ½-inch-thick rings

1 medium red bell pepper

Coarse salt

Freshly ground black pepper

¼ cup plus 2 tablespoons extra virgin olive oil, plus more for brushing the vegetables

1¼ cups Israeli couscous or regular couscous

2 tablespoons freshly squeezed lemon juice

1 small garlic clove, peeled and minced

1 cup small grape or pear tomatoes, halved

1 tablespoon chopped flat-leaf parsley

2 tablespoons basil chiffonade

Prepare an outdoor grill, letting the coals burn until they are covered with white ash.

Brush the zucchini, yellow squash, eggplant, onion rings, and bell pepper with a thin coat of olive oil, and season them with salt and pepper.

Grill the zucchini and yellow squash for 3 minutes on each side, turning them over once. Transfer them to a plate and set aside. Grill the eggplant until nicely caramelized and tender, about 4 minutes per side; then transfer it to the plate with the other vegetables. Grill the onions for 4 minutes on each side, and transfer them to the plate. Grill the bell pepper until all sides are charred, about 10 minutes. Put the pepper in a bowl and cover it with plastic wrap. Let it steam in its own heat for 10 to 15 minutes. Remove the pepper from the bowl and peel it. (The charred skin should come right off with the aid of a paring knife.) Cut it open and remove the seeds.

Cut all the vegetables into bite-size pieces and set them aside.

Bring a pot of lightly salted water to a boil over high heat. Add the couscous and cook until it is tender but still firm to the bite, 7 to 8 minutes. Drain, toss with the 2 tablespoons olive oil, and set aside.

In a small bowl, whisk together the lemon juice and garlic. Add the remaining ¼ cup olive oil. Season with salt and pepper.

In a large serving bowl, toss together the couscous, vegetables, tomatoes, parsley, and basil. Dress carefully with the vinaigrette, toss gently, and season with salt and pepper. Serve.

PAIRING

Grilled Swordfish with Summer Vegetable Compote (page 161)

FLAVOR BUILDING

Scallions and leeks, grilled and sliced, add great flavor to this salad.

FRISÉE SALAD WITH SMOKED BACON, SHIITAKES, AND AGED GOAT CHEESE

Based on the unassailable foundation of cool, crunchy, bitter greens and sautéed diced bacon, the classic frisée and lardon salad lends itself to a number of embellishments. Some restaurants top it with a poached egg; others add crumbled Roquefort, a rare instance in which all of the other ingredients are in a fair fight with the famously powerful blue cheese.

My version throws in another ingredient: shiitake mushrooms, which have a natural affinity with bacon and are among the best mushrooms for roasting. If you prefer creamy fresh goat cheese to the more pungent, dry, aged variety, that's fine; simply crumble it over the salad rather than passing it through a grater. SERVES 4

16 large shiitake mushrooms, stems removed

2/3 cup extra virgin olive oil

Coarse salt

Freshly ground black pepper

6 ounces slab bacon, cut crosswise into ¼-inch slices and then into ½-inch pieces (lardons)

2 teaspoons Dijon mustard

2 tablespoons red wine vinegar

6 cups frisée lettuce, curly endive, or Belgian endive leaves

2 tablespoons finely minced shallots

4 ounces aged (or fresh) goat cheese

Preheat the oven to 425°F.

Arrange the shiitakes on a roasting pan. Drizzle with 2 to 3 tablespoons of the olive oil, and season with salt and pepper. Roast in the oven for 8 to 10 minutes, until the mushrooms are soft, fragrant, and lightly browned. Remove them from the oven and when they are cool enough to handle, cut them into large pieces. Transfer them to a bowl and set aside.

Warm 1 teaspoon of the olive oil in a sauté pan set over medium heat. Add the bacon and sauté, stirring occasionally, until crisp, about 8 minutes. Remove it with a slotted spoon and set it on a paper towel–lined plate to drain. Reserve 2 tablespoons of the bacon fat and keep it warm.

In a bowl, mix together the mustard and vinegar, and season with salt and pepper. Whisk in the remaining olive oil and the reserved bacon fat. Taste and adjust the seasoning, adding a little more vinegar if the dressing seems oily.

Dress the mushrooms with about 1 tablespoon of the dressing and set aside. Put the lettuce in a salad bowl, add the mushrooms and shallots, and dress them lightly with the remaining vinaigrette. Grate half of the cheese (or crumble if using fresh) into the bowl, toss to combine, and season with salt and pepper. Scatter the bacon over the salad, and grate (or crumble) the remaining cheese over the top.

Serve family-style from a bowl or divide among four salad plates.

PAIRING

Sautéed Chicken Breasts with Button Mushrooms and Sage (page 164)

VARIATIONS

You can go a more traditional route and use blue cheese, ideally Roquefort, instead of the goat cheese.

Try sherry vinegar in place of the red wine vinegar.

FLAVOR BUILDING

A teaspoon of freshly chopped tarragon stirred into the dressing will complement all of the flavors here. Or whisk a tablespoon of honey into the dressing along with the mustard to subtly sweeten it.

FIG, PROSCIUTTO, AND ARUGULA SALAD WITH A BALSAMIC-HONEY DRIZZLE

I keep a small bottle of twenty-five-year-old balsamic vinegar on my kitchen counter and use this famously expensive condiment as sparingly as possible. But there comes a point at the end of each summer when I develop an appetite for a daily salad of tomatoes, scallions, fleur de sel, and balsamic vinegar. I began looking for a way to keep my balsamic "stash" from being depleted, and it occurred to me that mixing a less expensive balsamic vinegar with honey would temper the acidity and yield a sweetness and complexity that approximates the real thing, a theory that proved true. SERVES 4

2 tablespoons plus 1½ teaspoons balsamic vinegar

Coarse salt

Freshly ground black pepper

1 tablespoon honey

4 cups (loosely packed) arugula

1 tablespoon plus 1 teaspoon extra virgin olive oil

4 ounces prosciutto di Parma, thinly sliced (about 12 slices)

8 black or green figs, stems removed, sliced lengthwise

4 ounces goat cheese, crumbled, optional

Put the vinegar in a small bowl. Add a pinch of salt and a few grinds of pepper, and stir to dissolve them. Stir in the honey.

Put the arugula in another bowl, drizzle with the olive oil, and season with salt and pepper. Decoratively arrange the dressed arugula, the prosciutto, and figs over the surface of a serving platter. Crumble the goat cheese, if using, over the salad, and drizzle everything with the balsamic-honey dressing.

PAIRINGS

Steamed Leeks and Red Potatoes with Fresh Tomato Vinaigrette (page 37) and/or Preserved Tuna with Potatoes, Arugula, and Scallions (page 59)

VARIATIONS

Replace the figs with thin slices of ripe, soft, sweet Anjou pears and discover how well this fruit gets along with prosciutto and cheese.

Spanish Manchego is a good alternative to the goat cheese.

FLAVOR BUILDING

If you have a bottle of 20- to 50-year-old balsamic vinegar, enjoy it in this salad.

WATERMELON, CHERRY TOMATO, RED ONION, AND CUCUMBER SALAD

Our friends Toby and Lauren Cleaver own a lodge in Costa Rica that boasts one of the most spectacular settings in which I've ever eaten a meal, made even more memorable by the fact that we were there during Christmas week. The lodge's main dining room is nestled on the beach, yet within hiking distance of the rain forest.

Lauren, an accomplished cook, and her chef turn out some of the best food in the country. For one dinner we were served spicy grilled beef with a sweet, cooling accompaniment of watermelon, red onion, and cucumber dressed with olive oil and lime juice. Since this was a perfect antidote to the spicy beef, it occurred to me that it would also be a great dish with late-summer barbecues and picnics. SERVES 4

---

3 cups diced watermelon, preferably seedless (1-inch dice; see Note)

1 cup cherry tomatoes, halved

⅓ cup minced red onion

1 cup diced peeled, seeded cucumber (small dice)

3 tablespoons freshly squeezed lime juice, plus more to taste

2 tablespoons extra virgin olive oil

Coarse salt

Freshly ground black pepper

Put the watermelon, tomatoes, onions, cucumbers, lime juice, and oil in a large bowl. Season with salt and pepper and toss. Cover and chill in the refrigerator for at least 1 hour. Taste, and adjust the seasoning if necessary, adding some more lime juice if its flavor doesn't register. Serve well chilled.

Note: Seedless watermelon is produced from a hybrid seed developed in the 1950s. The benefits of seedless watermelon go beyond the convenience; because the flesh around seeds tends to soften, seedless watermelon is firmer.

PAIRING

Spicy Grilled Skirt Steak (page 181)

FLAVOR BUILDING

Diced red bell pepper and thinly sliced scallions (white part only) impart a taste reminiscent of gazpacho.

Crumbling some feta cheese over this salad adds a nice salty counterpoint.

CRISP VEGETABLE SALAD WITH SUNFLOWER SEEDS AND MUSTARD VINAIGRETTE

I suggest that you treat this recipe as a blueprint. These are among my favorite raw vegetables, but you could certainly replace a few of them with your own. That said, don't lose the radishes, which contribute an important, gently peppery heat, or the sunflower seeds, which add a nutty flavor. SERVES 4

3 tablespoons unsalted sunflower seeds

1 tablespoon Dijon mustard

3 tablespoons red-wine vinegar

2/3 cup extra virgin olive oil

Coarse salt

Freshly ground black pepper

1 large carrot, peeled and cut into medium dice

2 stalks celery, peeled and cut into medium dice

1 cucumber, peeled, seeded, and cut into medium dice

1/2 head cauliflower, separated into small florets (about 1 cup florets)

1 small jicama, cut into 1-inch medium dice

4 cups tender watercress leaves

4 large radishes, shaved on a mandoline or very thinly sliced with a sharp knife

Preheat the oven to 350 F. Spread out the sunflower seeds on a cookie sheet and roast until fragrant, about 5 minutes. Remove the sheet from the oven and let the seeds cool.

In a small bowl, whisk together the mustard and vinegar. Add the oil a drop at a time, whisking as you do. Season with salt and pepper.

In a bowl, toss together the carrot, celery, cucumber, cauliflower, jicama, sunflower seeds, watercress, and radishes. And the dressing, toss, and season with salt and pepper.

Serve the salad family-style from the center of the table.

FLAVOR BUILDING

Add 1/4 cup of one or more types of chopped herbs (parsley, chive, basil, mint), 1/2 cup thinly sliced red onion, and/or 1/2 cup thinly sliced scallions, white part plus 1 inch green part, to the salad just before tossing.

JICAMA SALAD WITH SHERRY-LIME VINAIGRETTE

My longtime chef de cuisine, Jacinto Guadarrama, a native of Mexico, often makes this jicama salad for the Gotham staff dinner. I love it for its diversity of flavors and textures, all of which seem made for each other. Sherry vinegar, lime juice, haricots verts, jicama, and tomatoes come together in a juicy, crunchy salad tinged with the spice of ancho chile and the heat of radishes. I sometimes use smoked paprika, an option included in the recipe. SERVES 4

Coarse salt

8 ounces haricots verts or regular green beans, ends trimmed

2 tablespoons freshly squeezed lime juice

2 tablespoons sherry vinegar

½ teaspoon ancho chile powder, smoked paprika, or paprika with a pinch of cayenne

Freshly ground black pepper

3 tablespoons extra virgin olive oil

8 ounces jicama, peeled and julienned (about 2 cups)

8 radishes, julienned, ideally on a mandoline (about ½ cup), green tops reserved

1 Roma (plum) tomato, peeled, seeded, and diced

2 cups watercress, tough stems removed (from about 1 bunch)

Bring a small pot of salted water to a boil. Fill a large bowl halfway with ice water. Add the haricots verts to the boiling water and cook them for 3 minutes. Drain, and cool them in the ice water. Drain again and set aside.

Make the vinaigrette: Whisk the lime juice, sherry vinegar, and ancho powder together in a small bowl, and season with salt and pepper. Slowly whisk in the olive oil.

In a large bowl, combine the jicama, radishes, haricots verts, and tomato. Dress with a few spoonfuls of the vinaigrette and season with salt and pepper. Arrange the salad on a serving platter. In the same bowl, dress the watercress and reserved radish leaves with the remaining vinaigrette, and season with salt and pepper. Garnish the vegetables with a bouquet of these dressed greens, and serve.

PAIRING

Pizza with Roasted Chiles, Manchego, and Scallions (page 101)

GRILLED PORTOBELLOS, OAK-LEAF LETTUCE, AND TOASTED WALNUTS

Mushrooms have a great affinity with sherry vinegar, but when dressed they have a tendency to absorb it, becoming too sharp and acidic. This recipe includes sweet balsamic vinegar to balance the flavor of the sherry. Of equal note is the use of the juice given off by the mushrooms as they rest after grilling. Stirred into the vinaigrette, it pulls the salad together. SERVES 4

2 tablespoons balsamic vinegar

1 tablespoon sherry vinegar

1 teaspoon Dijon mustard

1 teaspoon minced shallot

Coarse salt

½ cup plus 2 tablespoons extra virgin olive oil

Freshly ground white pepper

3 large or 4 medium portobello mushrooms, stems trimmed if necessary

8 cups mixed baby lettuces, such as red oak-leaf, green oak-leaf, and Bibb

⅓ cup grated Parmigiano-Reggiano

½ cup walnut halves, toasted and coarsely chopped

Prepare an outdoor grill, letting the coals burn until they are covered with white ash.

In a small bowl, whisk together the balsamic and sherry vinegars, mustard, shallots, and a pinch of salt. Slowly whisk in the ½ cup olive oil, then season to taste with more salt and pepper.

Brush the mushrooms with the remaining 2 tablespoons olive oil, and season them with salt and pepper. Grill them for 3 minutes on each side. Set the mushrooms in a bowl to catch their juices as they cool.

When the portobellos are cool, slice them into thick strips, and place them in a bowl. Whisk the accumulated mushroom juice into the vinaigrette.

Use about 2 tablespoons of the vinaigrette to dress the mushrooms. In another bowl, toss the lettuces with a few tablespoons of the vinaigrette, half of the cheese, and salt and pepper to taste. If necessary, add more vinaigrette and toss again. (You may not use all the vinaigrette.)

To serve, arrange the mushrooms and greens on a large serving platter. Scatter the chopped walnuts and the remaining cheese over the top.

PAIRING

Grilled Marinated Pork Chops (page 176)

VARIATIONS

For a more understated effect, use toasted pine nuts in place of the walnuts.

Shiitakes would be a good replacement for the portobello mushrooms.

FLAVOR BUILDING

Make the walnut flavor more prominent by replacing the olive oil with a high-quality imported walnut oil.

Crumble fresh goat cheese over the salad instead of tossing in Parmigiano-Reggiano.

FINGERLING POTATO SALAD WITH MUSSELS, FENNEL, AND SAFFRON

Mussels can be a powerful source of flavor. In this potato salad, their juices are concentrated by reducing them and using them in the aïoli dressing, allowing their briny flavor to permeate the dish. Similarly, you can make the fennel more dominant by using anise-flavored Pernod in place of the white wine to steam the mussels. SERVES 4

Coarse salt

2 stalks celery, peeled and halved crosswise

12 ounces fingerling or small Red Bliss potatoes

2 tablespoons extra virgin olive oil

1 small onion, peeled and cut into large dice (about ¾ cup diced)

½ fennel bulb, trimmed, cored, and cut into large dice (about ½ cup diced)

Pinch of saffron threads

2¼ teaspoons minced garlic (from about 2 cloves)

3 pounds mussels, preferably Prince Edward Island mussels, scrubbed

Freshly ground black pepper

½ cup dry white wine

⅔ cup mayonnaise, homemade (recipe follows) or store-bought

2 teaspoons freshly squeezed lemon juice

Pinch of cayenne pepper

2 tablespoons chopped flat-leaf parsley

Bring a saucepan of salted water to a boil. Fill a large bowl halfway with ice water. Add the celery to the boiling water and blanch it for 1 minute. Transfer the celery to the ice water to stop the cooking. Pat the celery dry and cut it into medium dice. Set aside.

Put the potatoes in a saucepan and cover them with water. Salt the water and set the pot over high heat. Cook until the potatoes are done (a sharp, thin-bladed knife will pierce easily to the center), approximately 15 minutes. While they are cooking, prepare the rest of the dish.

Heat the olive oil in a large pot set over medium heat. Add the onions and fennel, and sauté until softened but not browned, about 5 minutes. Add the saffron and 2 teaspoons of the garlic, and sauté for 1 minute. Add the mussels and a few grinds of pepper, and stir.

Raise the heat to high, add the wine, cover, and steam until the mussels open, about 5 minutes. Remove the pot from the heat and remove the mussels from the pot with a slotted spoon, discarding any that have not opened. Let them cool. Remove the mussels from

their shells and set them aside, lightly covered with plastic wrap.

Strain the mussel cooking liquid through a fine-mesh strainer set over a small pot. Set aside the solids and set the pot over high heat. Bring the liquid to a boil and continue to boil until reduced to 2 tablespoons, 5 to 10 minutes. Remove the pot from the heat and pour the liquid into a small bowl, scraping the sides of the pot with a rubber spatula to remove as much liquid as possible. Set the bowl aside to let the liquid cool.

By now the potatoes should be just about done. When they are, drain them in a colander and set them aside to cool briefly. When they are cool enough to handle but still warm, slice them crosswise into ¼-inch rounds, put them in a bowl, and season with salt and pepper. Add the mussels and reserved onions, fennel, and celery, and set aside.

In a small bowl, whisk together the mayonnaise and lemon juice; then whisk in the reduced mussel cooking liquid. Stir in the remaining ¼ teaspoon garlic, the cayenne, and the parsley, and season with salt and pepper.

MAYONNAISE

Add about three-quarters of the dressing to the bowl with the mussels and vegetables, and toss. The salad should be lightly but evenly coated; if not, add a bit more dressing and toss again.

Divide the salad among individual plates, and serve.

FLAVOR BUILDING

This is an easy dish to alter: Add some dried orange peel to the mussels' cooking liquid for a bouillabaise-like flavor. Or replace the parsley with cilantro.

2 large egg yolks, at room temperature

About 2 tablespoons freshly squeezed lemon juice

1 tablespoon Dijon mustard

Coarse salt to taste

Freshly ground white pepper to taste

Cayenne pepper to taste

1 cup olive oil

1 cup canola oil

Put the egg yolks, lemon juice, mustard, salt, white pepper, and cayenne in a medium bowl and whisk them together with a whisk or an immersion blender. Add the oils, drop by drop, whisking as you do. As the mayonnaise begins to thicken, add the oils a bit more quickly. When all of the oil has been absorbed, taste and add more lemon juice, salt, or pepper if necessary. This mayonnaise may be kept, covered, in the refrigerator for up to 2 days.

NANTUCKET BAY SCALLOP CEVICHE WITH SUNCHOKES, RADISH GREENS, AND CORIANDER SEEDS

In a true ceviche, raw fish or shellfish is marinated for a period of time in a highly acidic dressing that "cooks" it. In this loose adaptation, scallops and vegetables are tossed with a subtler lime vinaigrette immediately before serving, which preserves the unique, almost candylike sweetness of the raw Nantucket Bay scallops.

   As with any raw seafood preparation, it's crucial to maintain the freshness of the ingredients, so keep the scallops well chilled in the refrigerator until you're ready to toss and serve the ceviche, and be sure to chill the martini glasses in the refrigerator as well for a few minutes. SERVES 4

3 tablespoons extra virgin olive oil

About 2 tablespoons freshly squeezed lime juice plus finely grated zest of 1 lime

1/4 teaspoon ground coriander seeds

2 medium red radishes, leafy greens intact

1 pound Nantucket Bay scallops

2 medium sunchokes (also known as Jerusalem artichokes), peeled and cut into a fine julienne

Coarse salt

Freshly ground white pepper

2 teaspoons minced chives

Put the oil, 1½ tablespoons lime juice, lime zest, and coriander seeds into a small bowl and whisk together to make a vinaigrette. Taste and add a few more drops of lime juice, if necessary. Set aside.

Cut the radish greens from the radishes. Wash them, spin them dry, and roughly chop them. Thinly slice the radishes with a thin-bladed knife or Japanese mandoline. Stack the slices and cut them into a fine julienne. Put the radishes and greens in a bowl and add the scallops and sunchokes. Season with salt and pepper. Drizzle the vinaigrette over the scallops and vegetables and gently toss. Add the chives and gently toss again.

Divide the ceviche among four chilled martini glasses and serve at once.

PAIRING

Sautéed Chicken Breasts with Button Mushrooms and Sage (page 164)

VARIATION

If you can't find radishes with vibrant, leafy greens intact, substitute ½ cup roughly chopped watercress.

SPICY SHRIMP SALAD WITH MANGO, AVOCADO, AND LIME VINAIGRETTE

I improvised this dish of grilled marinated prawns as a contribution to a late-summer dinner party. The mango and avocado in the salad have a cooling effect that mitigates the heat of the paprika and cayenne pepper. SERVES 4

1½ pounds extra-large shrimp (3 to 4 per person), peeled and deveined

½ cup plus 2 tablespoons grapeseed oil

3 garlic cloves, peeled and finely chopped

2 tablespoons smoked paprika

¼ teaspoon plus a pinch of cayenne pepper

1 heaping tablespoon finely grated orange zest

1 tablespoon coarsely cracked black pepper

¼ cup freshly squeezed lime juice, plus 1 generous teaspoon grated lime zest

½ teaspoon Dijon mustard

1 teaspoon coarse salt, plus more to taste

¼ cup extra virgin olive oil

Freshly ground white pepper to taste

½ small red onion, halved, peeled, and thinly sliced (about ⅓ cup sliced)

1 mango, peeled, seeded, and cut into ½-inch dice

1 avocado, peeled, pitted, and cut into ½-inch dice

4 cups (loosely packed) soft lettuces, such as Red Oak or Lolla Rossa

Put the shrimp in a bowl.

Make the marinade: Pour ¼ cup of the grapeseed oil into a small bowl. Add the garlic, paprika, ¼ teaspoon cayenne pepper, orange zest, and cracked black pepper, and stir together. Set aside 1 tablespoon of the mixture, and pour the remaining marinade over the shrimp. Toss, cover, and refrigerate for 30 minutes to 6 hours.

Make the vinaigrette: In a small bowl, whisk together the reserved 1 tablespoon marinade, the lime juice and zest, the mustard, 1 teaspoon salt, and the remaining pinch of cayenne. Slowly whisk in the remaining ¼ cup grapeseed oil, then the olive oil. Season to taste with salt and white pepper.

Put the onion, mango, avocado, and lettuces in a large bowl. Dress lightly with ½ cup of the vinaigrette, or more if necessary, and season with salt and white pepper. (Extra dressing can be spooned over the shrimp.) Set aside.

Heat the remaining 2 tablespoons grapeseed oil in a sauté pan set over medium-high heat. Season the shrimp with salt, add them to the pan, and sear quickly, just over 1

minute on each side. Remove them from the pan and cover to keep warm.

Mound the salad in the center of a platter and surround it with the shrimp. Serve family-style from the center of the table, passing any extra dressing alongside.

PAIRING

Grilled Swordfish with Summer Vegetable Compote (page 161)

VARIATIONS

At the Gotham, we serve a version of this dish using grilled Spanish mackerel.

Sliced scallions (white parts only) would be a fine alternative to the red onion in the salad.

FLAVOR BUILDING

Try diced papaya or pineapple in addition to the mango.

GRILLED MARINATED TUNA WITH PAPAYA AND GRILLED SCALLIONS

This list of Asian ingredients is loaded with compelling contrasts: soy sauce balancing sugar in the marinade; lemon juice meeting peppery ginger in the vinaigrette; and crunchy, cool daikon sprouts on the finished plate. This can be served as a starter, and it is also an ideal summer lunch that can be pulled together very quickly, with the cooking taking just a few minutes on an outdoor grill. The versatile marinade is also delicious on bass, swordfish, or chicken breasts. SERVES 4

20 scallions

½ cup soy sauce, preferably whole bean

1½ teaspoons finely chopped garlic

1½ teaspoons finely chopped ginger

2 teaspoons sugar

4 tuna steaks, 6 ounces each

About 2 tablespoons freshly squeezed lemon juice

¼ cup plus 2 tablespoons extra virgin olive oil

Freshly ground black pepper to taste

Coarse salt to taste

1 papaya, peeled, seeded, and cut into medium dice

1 cup (loosely packed) daikon sprouts, radish sprouts, or mizuna

Cut off the scallion tops, leaving 1 inch of green. Set the scallion lengths aside. Chop enough of the trimmed tops to make ¼ cup.

Make the marinade: stir the soy sauce, garlic, ginger, sugar, and chopped scallion tops together in a glass or ceramic dish that is wide enough to hold the tuna in a single layer. Measure out 3 tablespoons of the marinade, leaving behind as many solids as possible, and set it aside for the vinaigrette. Add the tuna to the marinade, cover, and refrigerate for 1 to 4 hours, turning the tuna over periodically.

Prepare an outdoor grill for cooking, letting the coals burn until they are covered with white ash.

Make the vinaigrette: In a small bowl, whisk together the reserved 3 tablespoons marinade, 2 tablespoons lemon juice, and ¼ cup olive oil. Season to taste with pepper, and more lemon juice if necessary to balance the acidity, and set aside.

In a bowl, toss the scallion lengths with 1 tablespoon of the oil. Season with salt, place on the grill, and cook, turning often, until softened and lightly browned, 3 to 4 minutes. Transfer the scallions to a plate and set them aside.

Remove the tuna and brush off any remaining marinade. Drizzle the tuna with the remaining 1 tablespoon oil, season with salt and pepper, and place the pieces on the grill. Grill, turning once, for approximately 4 minutes for rare, 5 minutes for medium rare, and 6 minutes for medium; times will vary based on the thickness of the fish.

To serve, cut the tuna into thick slices and divide the slices among four plates. Arrange the scallions, papaya, and sprouts on the plate with the tuna, and spoon some vinaigrette over each serving. Pass any extra vinaigrette alongside.

VARIATION

Use mango in place of the papaya.

FLAVOR BUILDING

Diced avocado, arranged on the plate along with the scallions, sprouts, and papaya, adds a creamy finish to this salad.

PRESERVED TUNA WITH POTATOES, ARUGULA, AND SCALLIONS

By preserved tuna, I mean the best canned or jarred tuna available, which usually comes from Italy or Spain, is packed in extra virgin olive oil, and is far superior to most supermarket brands. It's more expensive than American offerings, but its luscious texture and flavor more than make it worth it. (It's usually sold as "tuna preserved in oil"; a popular brand is Flott.) I've included a recipe for making your own, which is a fairly easy proposition.

The key to this dish's success is to toss everything together while the potatoes are warm; their heat helps the flavors meld and causes the arugula to wilt. SERVES 4

Coarse salt

1 pound fingerling or other waxy potatoes

1 tablespoon Dijon mustard

1 egg yolk, at room temperature

3 tablespoons freshly squeezed lemon juice

¾ cup grapeseed oil

½ teaspoon minced garlic

Grated lemon zest to taste, optional

Freshly ground black pepper

2 cups (loosely packed) arugula, chopped

One 8-ounce jar preserved tuna (Spanish or Italian), or 8 ounces homemade preserved tuna (recipe follows), drained, in chunks

¼ cup Kalamata olives, pitted and cut into slivers

2 teaspoons capers, rinsed and drained

About 4 scallions, white part and 1 inch of green, thinly sliced on the diagonal (⅓ cup sliced)

Fleur de sel

Bring a pot of lightly salted water to a boil. Add the potatoes and simmer for 12 to 15 minutes. (They are done when a sharp, thin-bladed knife easily pierces through to their center.)

While the potatoes are cooking, make the vinaigrette: Put the mustard, egg yolk, and lemon juice in a bowl and whisk them together. Slowly add the oil in a thin stream, whisking to form an emulsion. Stir in the garlic, and the lemon zest if using, and season to taste with salt and pepper. Set aside.

When the potatoes are done, drain them and let them cool slightly. When they are cool enough to handle (but still very warm), cut them crosswise into ½-inch-thick rounds. Put the slices in a salad bowl. Add the vinaigrette, arugula, tuna, olives, capers, and scallions. Toss. Taste, and adjust the seasoning with fleur de sel, pepper, and more lemon juice, if necessary. If desired, you can increase the salinity by adding more capers as well. Serve warm or at room temperature.

PAIRINGS

Steamed Leeks and Red Potatoes with Fresh Tomato Vinaigrette (page 37) and/or Fig, Prosciutto, and Arugula Salad with Goat Cheese and a Balsamic-Honey Drizzle (page 43)

VARIATION

Substitute cooked penne, farfalle (bow-tie pasta), or white beans for the potatoes.

FLAVOR BUILDING

Adding chopped anchovy, minced garlic, and/or chopped parsley to the dressing will punch up the flavor.

PRESERVED TUNA

If you'd like to make your own preserved tuna, here's a recipe for doing so. If possible, purchase tuna cut from the belly section, which has a relatively high fat content. You will need a clip-on frying thermometer for this recipe. MAKES 1 POUND

2 thick tuna steaks, 8 ounces each, preferably bluefin

About 1 cup extra virgin olive oil

Chopped zest of 1 lemon with no pith whatsoever

2 garlic cloves, peeled and thinly sliced

1 tablespoon thyme leaves, coarsely chopped (from about 3 sprigs)

1 bay leaf, crumbled

2 teaspoons coarse salt, plus more for seasoning the fish

2 teaspoons cracked white pepper

Brush the tuna with a little of the olive oil. In a bowl, stir together the lemon zest, garlic, thyme, bay leaf, 2 teaspoons salt, and the pepper, and coat the tuna with the mixture. Wrap the tuna snugly in plastic wrap and let it marinate in the refrigerator for 4 to 6 hours.

Twenty minutes before cooking, remove the tuna from the plastic wrap, season it with coarse salt, and put it in a pan that is just large enough to hold it snugly. Cover it with the remaining oil. Let sit for 20 minutes. Then set the pan over very low heat and slowly bring the oil to 165°F.

Remove the pan from the heat and allow the tuna to cool to room temperature. Remove the tuna from the oil and brush off the marinade. Fit the tuna into a container that is just large enough to hold the fish, breaking it into large pieces if necessary. (A wide-mouth jar works well.) Strain the oil into the jar. Cover tightly and store in the refrigerator for at least 2 days. It will keep for up to 4 days.

Before serving, let the tuna come to room temperature.

HONEY-GINGER GLAZED QUAIL
ON WILTED LETTUCES

I don't generally eat a lot of spicy food, but I've always been fascinated by those masochists who thrive on it. Occasionally, though, I do find myself craving some heat, eating spicy dishes day after day. This is a distinctly Asian recipe that I developed when in that mindset. It balances honey and soy sauce and gets most of its heat from the serrano chile, a small pepper that packs a big, spicy wallop. Chiles are capsicum peppers, which cause the nervous system to produce endorphins (the same reaction causes "runner's high"). In other words, to some extent, they're addictive.

This quail also pairs very well with the mango and avocado salad on page 54. SERVES 4

---

3 tablespoons soy sauce

5 tablespoons honey

3 garlic cloves peeled and minced, plus 2 garlic cloves, crushed with the side of a knife and peeled

1 teaspoon thinly sliced serrano chile pepper

2 tablespoons chopped ginger

1 teaspoon freshly ground black pepper, plus more to taste

1 tablespoon grated orange zest, plus ½ cup freshly squeezed orange juice

¼ teaspoon ground cardamom

2 tablespoons grapeseed oil

4 quail, boned

¼ cup rice wine vinegar

2 tablespoons freshly squeezed lime juice

2 tablespoons extra virgin olive oil

6 cups watercress (from about 3 bunches, large stems removed)

Coarse salt

In a bowl, stir together the soy sauce, honey, minced garlic, sliced chile, ginger, 1 teaspoon pepper, orange zest, cardamom, and grapeseed oil. Put the quail in a baking dish and pour the marinade over it. Cover and let marinate in the refrigerator for 1 to 4 hours.

When ready to proceed, preheat the oven to 375°F. Remove the quail from the marinade and set them aside. Strain the marinade through a fine-mesh strainer set over a bowl. Discard the solids.

Stir the vinegar, orange juice, and lime juice into the strained marinade, and pour the mixture into a saucepan. Set the pan over high heat, bring to a boil, and cook until reduced to a glaze, approximately 15 minutes.

Heat an ovenproof sauté pan over medium-high heat. Add the quail, skin side down, and cook for 2 to 3 minutes. Turn the birds over, brush them with the glaze, and transfer the pan to the oven. Bake for 3 minutes. Brush with the glaze again and set the pan aside.

Pour the olive oil into a sauté pan and heat it over medium-high heat. Add the crushed garlic and sauté until golden brown, approximately 3 minutes. Add the watercress, season with salt and pepper, and sauté just until wilted, approximately 1½ minutes.

To serve, mound some watercress in the center of each of four dinner plates, and place a quail on top.

PAIRING

Sautéed Spinach with Garlic, Ginger, and Sesame Oil (page 199)

FARRO, CHICKEN, AND AVOCADO SALAD WITH LIME VINAIGRETTE

This recipe uses the Italian grain farro, known in the United States as spelt, which has been popular in Tuscany for centuries and today can be found in many American supermarkets and almost any health food store. Its nutty flavor lends itself to hot and cold applications—you're as apt to find it cooked, cooled, and tossed into a salad as you are to encounter it in *farrotto,* an alternative to risotto. Don't opt for a smaller grain here; farro's size is crucial to its remaining pleasingly toothsome after it's dressed with the vinaigrette. SERVES 4

VINAIGRETTE

1 teaspoon finely chopped garlic

3 tablespoons freshly squeezed lime juice

1 tablespoon minced, seeded jalapeño pepper (about 1 pepper)

½ cup extra virgin olive oil

Coarse salt

Freshly ground black pepper

SALAD

½ cup farro

1 tablespoon extra virgin olive oil

Coarse salt

Freshly ground black pepper

3 boneless, skinless chicken breasts (about 1 pound total)

2 cups Chicken Stock, cold (page 31)

2 ripe avocados, peeled and sliced lengthwise

1 red bell pepper, seeds and stem removed, cut into small dice

2 heads Boston or Bibb lettuce, torn into bite-size pieces

½ cup thinly sliced red onion

2 tablespoons cilantro leaves, plus 8 sprigs

Make the vinaigrette: In a small bowl, whisk together the garlic, lime juice, jalapeño, and olive oil. Season to taste with salt and pepper. Set it aside.

Bring 1 quart of salted water to a boil in a pot set over high heat. Add the farro and cook until it is tender but still toothsome, about 30 minutes. Strain the farro, transfer it to a bowl, toss it with the oil, and season to taste with salt and pepper.

Put the chicken and stock in a pot, season with salt and pepper, and slowly bring the stock to a boil over high heat. Lower the heat and simmer until the chicken is just cooked, 12 to 15 minutes. Drain, reserving the stock for another use, and set the chicken aside.

Thickly slice the chicken crosswise; add the avocado, bell pepper, lettuce, onion, and cilantro leaves to the bowl with the farro. Add the chicken and the vinaigrette. Toss, and transfer the salad to a large serving bowl. Garnish with the cilantro sprigs and serve.

SOUPS, SANDWICHES, AND PIZZAS

SOUPS, SANDWICHES, AND PIZZAS CAN BE AS SOPHISTICATED
and satisfying as other main course dishes. Too many people look at these categories casually and tend to
put them together without using much creativity. It might inspire you to know that preparing
memorable soups, sandwiches, and pizzas isn't much more taxing than making more predictable ones—
they are all, almost by definition, some of the easiest things to cook. They are also very convenient:
Most soups can be made well in advance and kept refrigerated for days. And because of their inherent
simplicity, pizzas can be prepared on a few minutes' notice. Here are some guidelines for thinking about
soups, sandwiches, and pizzas:

SOUPS

Food should respect the seasons as much as possible, which is probably why I love soups: They make
some of the strongest seasonal statements in a kitchen.

At the forefront of most of the soups in this chapter is a single ingredient or pair of ingredients that
unmistakably belong to a particular season. In the fall, for example, I'm apt to make Kabocha Squash
Soup with Ginger, Fenugreek, Apple, and Pumpkin Seeds or Roasted Chestnut Soup. And in the dead of
winter, I can't think of anything more warming and restorative than Rich Short Rib Soup.

In keeping with one of this book's themes, some recipes here draw on international inspiration, such
as the fragrant Lamb and Chickpea Soup and the Pumpkin and Caramelized Onion Soup with Gruyère
and Sage, a new take on the traditional French onion soup.

SANDWICHES

There are just three sandwiches in this chapter, but each offers lessons beyond the recipe itself. The Grilled Vegetable, Arugula, and Fresh Mozzarella Sandwich gives a good indication of the possibilities of open-face sandwiches, and can certainly be adapted to include other vegetables, greens, and cheeses. The Roast Turkey, Avocado, Bacon, and Blue Cheese Sandwich borrows Cobb salad ingredients to illustrate how effective it is to reimagine dishes in new ways, and shares a useful recipe for brined turkey. And the Turkey Burger is founded on a technique for replicating the texture of a beef burger in a more healthful context.

PIZZA

When it comes to pizza, everyone is an expert. One's preference for thin or thick crust, amount of cheese, and choice of toppings isn't usually based on an authoritative knowledge. Rather, it's founded on personal favorites and fond taste memories.

Recently I've become a big fan of grilled pizzas as much for their convenience as for their flavor. Pizza dough can be purchased from a pizzeria and is available in supermarkets; it can be rolled out and grilled in advance. When the time comes to serve it, all you need to do is add the topping and bake it in the oven, making pizza-making a fun, surprisingly easy diversion for the family or a large group.

BROCCOLINI SOUP WITH CRÈME FRAÎCHE AND GARLIC CROUTONS

You might have noticed broccolini, a long-stemmed, green vegetable with bushy little florets at the top, in the supermarket alongside broccoli and broccoli rabe. Broccolini—also known as Asperation or baby broccoli—is a recently developed hybrid of broccoli and Chinese kale. I find it appealing for its deep green hue and for a flavor that is at once more refined than broccoli's and less bitter than broccoli rabe's. Here this vegetable is the basis for a pureed soup, where it's balanced with crème fraîche and herbed garlic croutons. Finely chopping the broccolini allows it to cook quickly, thereby preserving all of its brilliant color. SERVES 4

2 tablespoons extra virgin olive oil

4 garlic cloves, crushed with the side of a knife and peeled

¼ loaf firm, white sandwich bread, crusts removed, sliced ¼ inch thick and cut into small dice (about 1 cup diced)

¼ teaspoon chopped thyme leaves

Coarse salt

Freshly ground black pepper

1 tablespoon canola oil

½ cup finely chopped onion

¼ cup finely chopped celery

½ cup diced peeled Yukon Gold potato (½-inch dice)

1 quart Chicken Stock (page 31)

4 cups finely chopped broccolini (¼-inch pieces, from about 3 bunches)

2 tablespoons unsalted butter

¼ cup crème fraîche

Preheat the oven to 325°F.

Heat 1 tablespoon of the olive oil in an ovenproof sauté pan set over medium heat. Add half the garlic and sauté for 4 minutes. Add the bread, thyme, and remaining 1 tablespoon olive oil, season with salt and pepper, and stir. Transfer the pan to the oven and cook, stirring regularly, until the bread is crisp all over, about 15 minutes. Remove the pan from the oven and let cool. These croutons can be kept in an airtight container at room temperature for up to 1 week, but be sure to remove the garlic before storing them.

Heat the canola oil in a large, heavy-bottomed pot set over medium heat. Add the onion and celery, and sauté for 4 minutes without browning. Add the remaining garlic and the potatoes, and cook for 6 more minutes. Add the stock, season with salt and pepper, and bring to a boil over high heat.

With the stock at a full boil, add the broccolini. Continue cooking until it is just tender, about 4 minutes.

While the soup is cooking, fill a large bowl halfway with ice water.

Pour the soup into a bowl and set the bottom half of the bowl into the ice bath. Stir the soup with a spoon to release the heat and cool it as quickly as possible, which will help maintain its dark green color.

Strain the soup through a fine-mesh strainer set over a bowl, reserving the solids and liquid separately. Working in batches if necessary, put the solids in a blender and process, adding some of the liquid until the mixture takes on a uniformly thick, smooth consistency.

Return the soup to the pot, stir in enough of the remaining liquid to maintain a thick consistency, and gently reheat it.

The soup can be made to this point, cooled, covered, and refrigerated for up to 3 days. Reheat gently before proceeding.

Swirl in the butter, and season the soup with salt and pepper.

To serve, ladle some soup into each of four shallow warmed bowls, and garnish each serving with a swirl of crème fraîche and a scattering of croutons.

PAIRING

Braised Pork with Fennel and Red Bliss Potatoes (page 174)

VARIATIONS

Broccoli or broccoli rabe can be used in place of the broccolini.

The garlic croutons would be perfect on Fennel Soup (page 81).

This soup is also delicious cold.

FLAVOR BUILDING

Rather than using canola oil, begin the soup by slowly cooking minced bacon over low heat until it turns crisp and renders enough fat to coat the bottom of the pot. Remove the bacon with a slotted spoon and let it drain on a paper towel–lined plate. This will both impart a smoky undercurrent to the soup and provide an additional garnish; scatter some of the crisp bacon over the surface of each serving.

CARROT-SAFFRON SOUP WITH CRÈME FRAÎCHE

This soup started out as a sauce. I was intrigued by the way carrots and saffron interact, the elusive flavor of saffron tempering the sweetness of the carrot. (The deep golden-orange color they produce is a happy by-product.) Of course, saffron makes an unmistakable impact on everything it touches, a classic example being risotto ala Milanese, in which a few threads alter the nature of the entire dish. SERVES 6

1 tablespoon unsalted butter

¾ cup thinly sliced onion

¾ cup thinly sliced leek (white part plus 1 inch of green)

Pinch of saffron threads

Coarse salt

4 cups thinly sliced carrots (from about 5 medium carrots)

4½ cups Chicken Stock (page 31)

1 bouquet garni (1 bay leaf, 2 sprigs thyme, and 5 sprigs parsley, wrapped in a cheesecloth bundle and tied with kitchen string)

Freshly ground white pepper

6 tablespoons crème fraîche

Melt the butter in a large, heavy-bottomed pot set over medium heat. Add the onions and leeks, and sauté until softened but not browned, about 6 minutes. Add the saffron and a pinch of salt, stir, and cook for 2 minutes.

Add the carrots, stock, and bouquet garni. Raise the heat to high and bring the liquid to a boil. Reduce the heat, cover the pot, and simmer until the carrots are tender, about 35 minutes.

Working in batches if necessary, use a slotted spoon to transfer the carrots to a blender or food processor. Puree the carrots until they are smooth, and transfer them to a bowl.

Stir enough of the stock into the pureed carrots for the soup to have a thick consistency. You should have between 6 and 7 cups of soup. Season the soup with salt and pepper.

The soup can be made to this point, then cooled, covered, and refrigerated for up to 3 days. Reheat gently before proceeding.

To serve, ladle a cup or so of soup into each of six warmed bowls, and garnish each serving with a tablespoon of crème fraîche.

PAIRING

Roasted Wild Striped Bass with Leeks, Fingerling Potatoes, and Lemon (page 147)

VARIATION

This soup is also delicious cold.

FLAVOR BUILDING

Adding a teaspoon of grated ginger along with the saffron will bring a beguiling peppery flavor to the soup.

A great final flourish would be a teaspoon or two of grated orange zest stirred into the soup and a drizzle of orange oil scattered over the surface.

For a distinctly different soup, replace the saffron with 1 teaspoon curry powder and a pinch of cayenne pepper.

MUSSEL SOUP WITH SAFFRON, FENNEL, AND WHITE BEANS

Using Pernod instead of white wine or water is a simple way to transform basic steamed mussels into something compelling. As the mussels pop open, their juice is released into the liqueur, creating a complex and delicious broth. The sweet anise fragrance of the Pernod is compounded here by the addition of gently cooked fennel. Herbs and vegetables are added to the cooking liquid, which is finished with tomatoes, white beans, and a pinch of saffron. SERVES 6

¾ cup dried Great Northern beans

Coarse salt

Freshly ground black pepper

¼ cup olive oil

4 garlic cloves, peeled and minced

3 pounds mussels, preferably Prince Edward Island mussels, scrubbed and debearded

½ cup Pernod (see Note)

2 cups diced onions (from about 2 medium onions)

1¼ cups diced fennel (from about 1 medium bulb)

Pinch of saffron threads

2 cups chopped canned tomatoes, drained

Extra virgin olive oil

2 tablespoons chopped flat-leaf parsley

Soak the beans overnight in cold water to cover. Drain. Or use the quick-soak method (see page 30).

Put the beans in a large, heavy-bottomed pot. Add cold water to cover, by 2 inches and bring the water to a boil over high heat. Lower the heat and simmer for 30 minutes. Season the liquid with salt and pepper and continue to simmer until the beans are tender, about another 30 minutes. Drain the beans, reserving 2 cups of the cooking liquid.

Pour 2 tablespoons of the olive oil into a large, heavy-bottomed pot and add half the minced garlic. Set the pot over medium heat. When the garlic turns golden brown, add the mussels, stir, and add the Pernod. Raise the heat to high, bring the Pernod to a boil, and let boil for 1 minute. Then cover the pot and steam until the mussels open, 3 to 4 minutes. Remove the pot from the heat.

Use tongs to transfer the mussels to a bowl, discarding any that have not opened. Remove the mussels from their shells. Strain the liquid through a fine-mesh strainer set over a bowl. Reserve the liquid and

discard the solids. Rinse and dry the pot.

Pour the remaining 2 tablespoons olive oil into the pot and warm it over medium heat. Add the onions and cook until they are softened but not browned, about 4 minutes. Add the fennel and cook for another 8 minutes without browning the vegetables. Add the remaining garlic and the saffron, stir, and cook for 1 minute. Add the tomatoes, 1 cup of the reserved bean cooking liquid, and the reserved mussel liquid. Raise the heat to high and bring the liquid to a boil. Reduce the heat and simmer for 10 minutes. Add the beans and warm through. If the mixture seems too thick, add some more bean cooking liquid or water. Add the reserved mussels and let them warm through. Taste, and adjust the seasoning with salt and pepper if necessary.

To serve, ladle a cup or so of soup into each of six warmed bowls. Drizzle some extra virgin olive oil over the surface, and scatter the chopped parsley over each serving.

Note: Pernod is northern France's answer to pastis, a potent, anise-flavored spirit almost always diluted with water. All spirits belonging to this family are produced from either the actual licorice plant or anise and are often used in cooking to enhance fish dishes and soups.

VARIATIONS

Diced, cooked russet potatoes are a good, easy substitute for the beans.

If you're not a fan of Pernod, replace it with an equal quantity of white wine. To just tone down the Pernod influence, use white wine and finish the dish with a splash of Pernod.

FLAVOR BUILDING

Orange gets along very well with mussels and fennel; add dried orange peel to the mussels' cooking liquid.

CELERY ROOT AND CARAMELIZED PEAR SOUP

If ever there was a vegetable that proved that looks can be deceiving, it's knobby, homely celery root. Here, its understated celery flavor proves the perfect backdrop for sweet, honeyed pears. After sautéing the pears, the pan is deglazed with balsamic vinegar, resulting in a potent syrup that is drizzled over the soup just before serving. SERVES 6

4 tablespoons (½ stick) unsalted butter

1 cup sliced onion

¼ cup sliced celery

¼ cup thinly sliced leek, white part only, green top reserved for bouquet garni (see below)

2 garlic cloves, peeled and finely chopped

2½ cups chopped celery root (from about 3 small celery roots)

½ cup chopped Idaho potato

3 Bosc pears, peeled, cored, and cut into medium dice (about 1 cup diced), scraps reserved

4½ cups Chicken Stock (page 31)

1 bouquet garni (2 bay leaves, 5 sprigs parsley, and 2 sprigs thyme, wrapped together with the leek top and tied with kitchen string)

Coarse salt

Freshly ground white pepper

2 tablespoons honey

1 rosemary sprig

1 tablespoon balsamic vinegar

Melt 2 tablespoons of the butter in a large, heavy-bottomed pot set over medium heat. Add the onions, celery, and leeks, and sauté until softened but not browned, about 6 minutes. Add the garlic and cook for 1 minute. Add the celery root, potatoes, pear scraps, chicken stock, and bouquet garni. Raise the heat to high and bring the liquid to a boil. Season with salt and pepper, stir, reduce the heat, and cover. Cook at a simmer until the vegetables are tender, about 30 minutes.

Strain the soup through a fine-mesh strainer set over a bowl, reserving the solids and liquid separately. Working in batches if necessary, put the solids in a blender or food processor and puree, adding some of the liquid until the mixture takes on a uniformly thick, smooth consistency. Transfer the puree to a bowl.

Slowly stir in any remaining stock until the soup attains a thick, creamy consistency. Whisk in the remaining 2 tablespoons butter. You should have about 6 cups of soup. Season it with salt and pepper and set aside, covered, to keep warm.

Pour the honey into a sauté pan and warm it over medium-high heat until it bubbles and turns amber-colored, about 5 minutes. Add the diced pears and the rosemary sprig. Cook, tossing, until the pears are slightly softened and richly glazed. Add the balsamic vinegar and cook, tossing or stirring, for 2 minutes. Remove the pan from the heat, transfer the pears and sauce to a bowl and set aside, covered, to keep warm. (Discard the rosemary sprig.)

To serve, place a spoonful of pear in the center of each of six warmed soup plates. Ladle the soup around the pears, and drizzle the surface of each serving with the balsamic sauce.

PAIRING

Oxtail Braised in Red Wine with Mashed Root Vegetables (page 182)

VARIATION

If you prefer apples to pears, Granny Smiths are a perfect match for the celery root. Peel and dice 1 or 2 apples and sauté them briefly in butter. Leave out the honey, rosemary, and balsamic vinegar.

FLAVOR BUILDING

You can imitate a Gotham offering by placing a slice of seared foie gras in the center of each bowl, or by spreading some prepared foie gras terrine on a crouton and serving it alongside.

ROASTED CHESTNUT SOUP

Few flavors are as closely associated with a season as are chestnuts with winter, from the indelible musical mention of chestnuts roasting on an open fire to the woodsy, rustic flavor they add to classic holiday foods.

In many ways, a chestnut is more a vegetable than a nut. It has a high water content, which is why it's usually roasted; the cooking method extracts the chestnut's liquid and concentrates its flavor. It is also why chestnuts should be kept in the refrigerated section at the market, as opposed to the open air of the produce department (where they are usually found). Refrigeration keeps chestnuts from developing mold because of their moisture, or from drying out by losing it.

This recipe offers a sublime way to enjoy pure chestnut flavor in a pureed soup, where it's offset by sage and Brussels sprouts, not to mention the smoky undercurrent supplied by the bacon fat that serves as its starting point. Straining the soup makes it satiny while still retaining all of the chestnut flavor. SERVES 4 TO 6

---

16 chestnuts

1 large bone-in chicken breast (about 2 pounds), skin removed

Coarse salt

Freshly ground white pepper

4 ounces (4 strips) slab bacon, cut crosswise into ¼-inch slices and then into ½-inch pieces (lardons)

1 small onion, peeled and diced (about ¾ cup diced)

3 large garlic cloves, crushed with the side of a knife and peeled

3 tablespoons chopped sage leaves

¼ cup diced celery

1 bouquet garni (2 sprigs thyme and 1 bay leaf wrapped in a cheesecloth bundle and tied with kitchen string)

5 cups Chicken Stock (page 31)

12 Brussels sprouts, cored and separated into leaves (about 2 cups leaves)

1 carrot, peeled and cut into medium dice

Preheat the oven to 400°F.

Use a sharp, thin-bladed paring knife to score an X on the flat side of each chestnut. Spread the chestnuts out on a cookie sheet and roast them in the oven until fragrant, about 20 minutes, shaking the pan and stirring the chestnuts occasionally to prevent scorching and to ensure even cooking.

While the chestnuts are roasting, season the chicken with salt and pepper and set aside.

Put the bacon in a large, heavy-bottomed pot set over medium heat, and cook until browned, about 8 minutes. Use a slotted spoon to transfer the bacon to a paper towel–lined plate. Pour off and discard all but 2 tablespoons of the bacon fat in the pot.

Add the onions, garlic, sage, and celery to the pot and sauté for 5 minutes.

Meanwhile, peel the chestnuts and set 4 aside for garnish. Finely chop the remaining 12 chestnuts. Add the chopped chestnuts, the bouquet garni, the stock, and the chicken, bone side up, to the pot. Slowly bring the liquid to a boil. Cover the pot, lower the heat, and simmer for 15 minutes. When the chicken is done, use tongs or a slotted spoon to remove it from the pot, and set it aside to cool.

Skim any impurities that have risen to the surface of the liquid, and let it simmer for an additional 15 minutes. When the chicken is cool, cut it into small dice.

Meanwhile, bring a pot of salted water to a boil and fill a large bowl halfway with ice water. Cook the Brussels sprout leaves and the diced carrot in the pot just until tender, 1 to 2 minutes. Then use a slotted spoon to transfer them to the ice water to stop the cooking and preserve their color. Drain.

Coarsely chop the 4 reserved chestnuts. Working in batches if necessary, puree the soup in a blender. Strain it through a fine-mesh sieve into a saucepan, pressing down on the solids to extract as much liquid as possible. Return the soup to the stove, add the reserved chestnuts, bacon, diced chicken, Brussels sprout leaves, and carrots, and reheat gently until warmed through. Season with salt and pepper.

The soup can be made to this point, cooled, covered, and refrigerated for up to 3 days. Reheat gently before proceeding.

Ladle the soup into individual warmed bowls, and serve.

VARIATION

Duck breast would be a powerful alternative to the chicken.

FLAVOR BUILDING

Savoy cabbage, parsnip, celery root, and/or turnip, cooked in boiling salted water like the Brussels sprouts, would be good vegetables to add to this soup.

PUMPKIN AND CARAMELIZED ONION SOUP WITH GRUYÈRE AND SAGE

In this—my autumnal answer to the classic French onion soup—the traditional recipe is augmented with roasted pumpkin and an aromatic infusion of sage. But the presentation is as classic as it gets: the soup is poured into individual bowls and topped with cheese, which is melted under the broiler. (Note that you'll need heavy, flameproof ceramic soup bowls for this.)

Seek out, authentic Gruyère for this recipe. As with the classic onion soup, what tops the bowl is almost as important as what's in it. This recipe calls for chicken stock, but if you make or can purchase a good-quality beef or veal stock (the textbook choice), using it here will yield a significantly richer result. SERVES 4 TO 6

---

1 medium pumpkin or butternut squash (about 3 pounds), peeled, seeded, and cut into large dice

3 tablespoons unsalted butter, at room temperature

Coarse salt

Freshly ground black pepper

1½ medium onions, peeled and thinly sliced (about 3 cups sliced)

¼ cup thinly sliced celery

2 garlic cloves, peeled and minced

6 sage leaves, cut into a chiffonade

1 bay leaf

4½ cups Chicken Stock (page 31)

12 baguette slices, cut ½ inch thick (2 slices should fit snugly in each soup bowl), lightly toasted

About 8 ounces Gruyère cheese, grated

Preheat the oven to 450°F.

Put the pumpkin in an ovenproof sauté pan. Add 1 tablespoon of the butter, toss, and season with salt and pepper. Roast in the oven, stirring occasionally, until the pumpkin pieces are caramelized and beginning to soften, about 20 minutes.

Meanwhile, melt the remaining 2 tablespoons butter in a soup pot set over medium heat. Add the onions and cook slowly, stirring occasionally, until lightly browned, for 15 minutes. Season with salt and pepper. Add the celery, garlic, and sage, and cook for 2 minutes. Add the pumpkin, bay leaf, and stock, raise the heat to high, and bring to a boil. Reduce the heat, cover, and simmer for 15 minutes. Taste, and adjust the seasoning if necessary.

Preheat the broiler.

Put two ovenproof soup bowls on a cookie sheet. Ladle the soup into the bowls, and float 2 slices of toasted bread on top of each serving. Cover the toasts with a generous amount of Gruyère. Broil until browned and bubbly, about 3 minutes. Repeat with the remaining bowls, and serve.

VARIATIONS

Muenster and aged Gouda are good substitutes for the Gruyère.

A combination of the three cheeses would be pleasantly unique.

Kabocha and Hubbard squashes are suitable replacements for the pumpkin.

KABOCHA SQUASH SOUP WITH GINGER, FENUGREEK, APPLE, AND PUMPKIN SEEDS

Pumpkin soup is a ubiquitous offering at Caribbean restaurants, each of which prepares its own signature version. These soups achieve their flavor with a minimum of potent ingredients, especially fresh ginger and fenugreek, a light, pleasingly celery-like spice that's a component of most curry blends.

Kabocha belongs to the same family of squash as Hubbard, sugar pumpkin, and turban squash, all of which are less sweet than butternut or acorn. This quality makes it possible to attain a pleasing and complex range of flavors with relative ease. SERVES 4 TO 6

2 tablespoons unsalted butter

½ medium onion, peeled and coarsely chopped (about ⅔ cup chopped)

1 stalk celery, coarsely chopped (about ⅓ cup chopped)

1 tablespoon fenugreek seeds, ground

1 tablespoon grated ginger

1 garlic clove, peeled and finely chopped

¼ teaspoon ground cloves

1 large Kabocha squash (about 5 pounds), or 6 pounds Hubbard squash, peeled, seeded, and chopped into 2-inch pieces

1 quart Chicken Stock (page 31)

Coarse salt

Freshly ground white pepper

1 Granny Smith or other tart, crisp apple (green or red)

½ cup pumpkin seeds, toasted, optional

1 tablespoon finely chopped chives

Melt the butter in a large, heavy-bottomed pot set over medium heat. Add the onions and celery, and sauté until softened but not browned, about 5 minutes. Add the fenugreek, ginger, garlic, and cloves and sauté for 1 minute. Add the squash and stock, season lightly with salt and pepper, and raise the heat to high. Bring the stock to a boil, then cover, lower the heat, and simmer until the squash is tender, about 20 minutes.

Strain the soup through a fine-mesh strainer set over a bowl, reserving the solids and liquid separately. Working in batches if necessary, put the solids in a blender and process, adding some of the liquid until the mixture takes on a uniformly thick, smooth consistency. Season the soup with salt and pepper.

The soup can be made to this point, cooled, covered, and refrigerated for up to 3 days. Reheat gently before proceeding.

Peel the apple and cut it into small dice.

To serve, ladle the soup into warmed wide, shallow bowls and garnish each serving with a scattering of apple, pumpkin seeds if using, and chives.

PAIRING

Asian Striped Bass *en Papillote* (page 142)

VARIATION

Replace the fenugreek with ½ to 1 teaspoon curry powder for a more complex flavor.

FLAVOR BUILDING

Add as much heat as you like by sautéing some chile paste or crumbled dried chile along with the onion and celery.

Garnish each serving with chopped cilantro leaves and finely chopped scallions (white and light green parts only).

FENNEL SOUP

Fennel is one of those ingredients that has a polarizing effect: People either love it or hate it, with no middle ground.

I appreciate that there are so many ways to use fennel and all of its parts: In addition to the bulb, the stalks, which are too tough to eat, can be used to add great flavor to stock. This soup is thickened with heavy cream and pureed potato; the latter serves to soften the flavor. SERVES 4 TO 6

1 tablespoon unsalted butter

½ cup chopped onion

⅓ cup sliced celery

2 garlic cloves, crushed with the side of a knife and peeled

2 medium fennel bulbs, thinly sliced crosswise (about 4 cups sliced), plus 1 tablespoon chopped fennel fronds

½ cup diced russet or Idaho potato

Coarse salt

Freshly ground white pepper to taste

1 cup dry white wine

6 cups Chicken Stock (page 31)

½ cup heavy cream

Extra virgin olive oil

Melt the butter in a soup pot set over medium heat. Add the onions and celery and cook without browning for 6 minutes. Add the garlic, fennel, and potatoes. Season lightly with salt and pepper, and cook for 7 minutes. Add the wine and cook until it evaporates, about 5 minutes. Then add the stock and the cream, raise the heat to high, and bring the liquid to a boil. Lower the heat and simmer until the vegetables are tender, about 20 minutes.

Strain the soup through a fine-mesh strainer set over a bowl, reserving the solids and liquid separately. Puree the solids in a blender or food processor, adding some of the liquid until it's as thick as split-pea soup. You should have between 6 and 7 cups of soup. Season to taste with salt and pepper.

To serve, ladle the soup into individual warmed bowls and scatter some fronds over each serving.

PAIRING

Roast Cod with a New England Chowder Sauce (page 148)

FLAVOR BUILDING

For a more luxurious and substantial dish, enrich the soup by stirring in 2 tablespoons unsalted butter at the end, or by drizzling 2 tablespoons lemon oil over the surface before serving.

WHITE BEAN SOUP WITH
GARLIC AND ESCAROLE

At the Gotham Bar and Grill, we serve a pureed soup of white beans and slow-roasted garlic that we've garnished over the years with seared foie gras, seared diver scallops, Osetra caviar, or a drizzle of lemon oil. This soup is a stripped-down version of that one. The simple, classic pairing of escarole and white beans carries the day, feeling very satisfying and complete. SERVES 4

¾ cups dried Great Northern beans

3 tablespoons unsalted butter

½ cup onion, medium dice

6 cloves garlic, smashed and peeled

¼ cup celery, medium dice

2 medium leeks, white parts only, quartered and thinly sliced

5 cups Chicken Stock (page 31)

1 bay leaf

1 sprig of fresh thyme

Coarse salt

1 head escarole, quartered lengthwise with the root intact

2 tablespoons extra virgin olive oil, plus more for serving

Freshly ground white pepper to taste

Soak the beans overnight in enough cold water to cover them. Drain.

Melt 1 tablespoon of butter in a large, heavy-bottomed pot set over medium heat. Add the onion, garlic, celery, and leeks and sauté until softened but not browned, about 5 minutes. Add the beans, stock, bay leaf, and thyme and bring the liquid to a boil over high heat. Lower the heat, partially cover the pot, and let simmer until the beans are tender, about 50 minutes. While the beans are cooking, cook the escarole.

Bring a pot of salted water to a boil. Fill the bowl halfway with ice water. Add the escarole to the boiling water and cook until tender, about 2 minutes. Use tongs to transfer the escarole to the ice water to stop the cooking and preserve its color. Remove the escarole from the ice water and gently squeeze out the excess water. Coarsely chop the escarole, put it in a bowl, and toss it with the extra virgin olive oil. Season with salt and pepper and set aside.

When the beans are done, strain the contents of the pot through a fine-mesh strainer set over a bowl.

Fish out and discard the bay leaf and thyme. Working in batches if necessary, put the solids in a blender and process, adding liquid until the mixture takes on a uniformly thick and smooth consistency.

Pour the soup into a pot and set the pot over medium heat. Stir in enough of the liquid to reach a thick soup consistency, then swirl in the butter to enrich the soup, taste, and adjust the seasoning with salt and pepper. If necessary, rewarm the escarole in a sauté pan set over medium heat.

To serve, mound some escarole in the center of each of 4 warm soup plates. Ladle some soup around the escarole and drizzle each serving with extra virgin olive oil.

PAIRING

Sautéed Chicken Breasts with Button Mushrooms and Sage (page 164)

VARIATION

The escarole can be replaced by spinach.

FLAVOR BUILDING

For a more substantial dish, place a lightly seared sea scallop on top of the escarole in each bowl, drizzle the soup with lemon olive oil (page 14), and top each scallop with Osetra caviar.

To add a smoky undercurrent to the soup, begin the soup with diced bacon, following the instructions on page 76.

For a turnkey way of adding another dimension to this soup, simply replace the olive oil with a truffle oil or walnut oil.

LENTIL SOUP WITH SPINACH AND INDIAN SPICES

With its exotic spices, persistent heat, chopped spinach, and last-second addition of lemon juice, this soup tastes unmistakably Indian. That said, I've taken many liberties in fashioning the recipe, not least of which is the use of French green lentils (lentilles du Puy), which hold their shape better when cooked and have a finer flavor than traditional Indian lentils. SERVES 4 TO 6

2 tablespoons canola oil

1 cup finely diced onion

2 garlic cloves, peeled and minced

1 teaspoon grated ginger

2 green chile peppers, such as jalapeño, seeded and minced

4 teaspoons Madras curry powder

4½ cups Chicken Stock (page 31)

¾ cup French green lentils (lentilles du Puy)

Coarse salt

Freshly ground black pepper

4 cups (loosely packed) coarsely chopped spinach

1 tablespoon freshly squeezed lemon juice

1 tablespoon chopped cilantro leaves

3 tablespoons thinly sliced scallions, white and light green parts only

Heat the oil in a large, heavy-bottomed pot set over medium heat. Add the onions and cook until softened but not browned, 4 minutes. Add the garlic, ginger, half of the minced chile, and the curry powder. Cook for 2 more minutes over medium heat. Add the stock and lentils, raise the heat to high, and bring the liquid to a boil. Reduce the heat to low, partially cover the pot, and cook until the lentils are tender, 30 to 40 minutes. Season to taste with salt and pepper.

The soup can be made to this point, then cooled, covered, and refrigerated for up to 3 days. Reheat gently over low heat before proceeding.

Just before serving, raise the heat and add the spinach. Cook, stirring, until the spinach has wilted, about 1 minute. Stir in the lemon juice (to brighten and focus the flavors), then add the remaining minced chile.

To serve, divide the soup among individual warmed bowls. Sprinkle each serving with cilantro and scallions.

VARIATION

For a vegetarian version, substitute water or Vegetable Stock (recipe follows) for the chicken stock.

VEGETABLE STOCK

MAKES ABOUT 2 QUARTS

2 tablespoons olive oil

2 medium onions, peeled and thinly sliced

2 medium zucchini, thinly sliced

2 small leeks, split lengthwise, rinsed, and thinly sliced

1 medium fennel bulb, halved and thinly sliced

1 large beefsteak tomato, halved

1 whole garlic head, halved crosswise

2 large shallots, peeled and thinly sliced

Coarse salt to taste

2 thyme sprigs, coarsely chopped

2 basil sprigs, coarsely chopped

2 flat-leaf parsley sprigs, coarsely chopped

In a large saucepan, warm the oil over medium heat. Add the onions, zucchini, leeks, fennel, tomato, garlic, and shallots, and season with salt. Cover and cook until the vegetables are softened but not browned, approximately 10 minutes.

Add 2 quarts cold water and bring to a boil over high heat. Reduce the heat to medium-low and simmer, uncovered, for 20 minutes. Add the herbs and simmer for 10 minutes. Remove the pot from the heat and let steep for 10 minutes. Strain the stock into a large bowl or container, and cool completely.

Refrigerate for up to 3 days or freeze for up to 2 months.

WILD MUSHROOM MINESTRONE

"Minestone" usually refers to Italian soups featuring tomato, vegetables, beans, and pasta. They vary from household to household but traditionally feature a diverse mix of vegetables, no one more important than any other.

This minestrone focuses on fresh wild mushrooms, inviting you to select your own from among such irresistible candidates as morels, chanterelles, enoki, cèpes (porcini), hen-of-the-woods, and black trumpets. Choose one to emphasize its unique flavor, or use a mix for a more complex result. If you wish to purchase a store-bought organic mushroom stock and use it in place of the chicken stock, it would of course amplify the soup's theme even further. SERVES 4 TO 6

Coarse salt

4 ounces ditalini pasta

¼ cup extra virgin olive oil, plus more for drizzling on the soup

½ cup diced onion

¼ cup diced celery

¼ cup diced carrot

8 ounces mixed wild mushrooms

Freshly ground black pepper

1 teaspoon finely chopped garlic

½ cup canned whole tomatoes, drained and chopped

3½ cups Chicken Stock (page 31)

1 bouquet garni (1 bay leaf, 5 parsley sprigs, and 2 thyme sprigs wrapped in a cheesecloth bundle and tied with kitchen twine)

Scant ½ cup cooked Great Northern beans (from ⅓ cup dried beans)

1 tablespoon chopped flat-leaf parsley

2 tablespoons chopped basil

Bring a pot of salted water to a boil. Add the pasta and cook until al dente, about 10 minutes. Drain the pasta, transfer it to a bowl, and toss it with 2 tablespoons of the olive oil (to keep the pasta from sticking to itself).

Heat the remaining 2 tablespoons olive oil in a large, heavy-bottomed pot set over medium heat. Add the onion, celery, and carrot and sauté until softened but not browned, 6 minutes. Add the mushrooms, season with salt and pepper, and raise the heat to high. Cook for 4 minutes, stirring occasionally. Add the garlic and cook for 2 minutes. Add the tomatoes, stock, and bouquet garni. Bring the liquid to a boil, then reduce the heat and simmer, partially covered, for 25 minutes.

The soup can be made to this point, then cooled, covered, and refrigerated for up to 3 days. Wrap and refrigerate the beans and pasta in separate containers; let them come to room temperature before proceeding. Reheat the soup gently.

Add the beans and pasta to the pot, and cook until warmed through, approximately 2 minutes. Season to taste with salt and pepper. Stir the parsley and basil into the soup.

To serve, ladle the soup into individual warmed bowls, taking care to be sure each bowl has a good balance of vegetables and liquid. Drizzle with extra virgin olive oil, and serve at once.

PAIRINGS

Roasted Monkfish with Green Peppercorn Sauce (page 157), Filet Mignon with Madeira Sauce (page 178)

VARIATIONS

Since the primary flavor here is mushroom, Vegetable Stock (page 85) or water can be substituted for the chicken stock.

Fresh cranberry beans, fava beans, or shell beans can be substituted for the Great Northern beans.

FLAVOR BUILDING

The fresh mushrooms can be replaced by ½ ounce dried porcini, soaked in ½ cup hot water for 20 minutes, drained, and chopped.

Fresh sage, summer savory, lemon thyme, or marjoram can replace the basil and parsley.

Finish the soup with a grating of pecorino Romano cheese, a drizzle of porcini oil or white truffle oil, or a shaving of black truffle.

Add the rind of a piece of Parmigiano-Reggiano to the soup while it simmers.

LAMB AND CHICKPEA SOUP

I had my first taste of *harira* (lamb and chickpea soup), the national soup of Morocco, in one of the most colorful scenes I've ever witnessed: Every night the Marrakech town square, which serves as a market by day, is transformed into a combination strolling feast, bazaar, and three-ring circus. Vendors with rolling food carts sell local specialties, snake charmers and trained monkeys perform for the amusement of locals and visitors, and the atmosphere whips you into a trancelike state as you take in all of this activity.

On the night I visited the Marrakech bazaar, I sampled *harira* from a street vendor. The recipe featured here has no doubt been influenced by the rest of that dreamlike evening, so it may very well be a heartier, spicier version of the original. SERVES 4 TO 6

3 tablespoons canola oil

1 pound boneless lamb shoulder, cut into ½-inch cubes

Coarse salt

Freshly ground black pepper

2 tablespoons all-purpose flour

¾ cup chopped onion

½ cup chopped celery

2 teaspoons finely chopped garlic

1 teaspoon ground turmeric

½ teaspoon ground cumin

Pinch of saffron threads

½ teaspoon ground cinnamon

¼ teaspoon ground ginger

½ teaspoon cayenne pepper, optional

2 cups canned whole tomatoes, drained

1 tablespoon tomato paste

½ cup dried chickpeas

3 cups Chicken Stock (page 31)

1 tablespoon freshly squeezed lemon juice, plus more if needed

1 tablespoon chopped cilantro leaves

Heat 2 tablespoons of the oil in a large, heavy-bottomed pot set over medium heat. Season the lamb with salt and pepper, and dust it with the flour. Add the lamb to the pot and brown it on all sides, stirring, about 7 minutes. Remove the lamb from the pot and set it aside.

Add the remaining 1 tablespoon oil to the pot and let it heat for a minute or two. Add the onion and celery and cook without browning, stirring often, for 5 minutes. Add the garlic, turmeric, cumin, saffron, cinnamon, ginger, and, if desired, cayenne pepper. Cook for 1 minute. Add the tomatoes and tomato paste, scrape the bottom of the pot to loosen any flavorful bits, and cook for 1 minute.

Add the chickpeas, lamb, and chicken stock. Raise the heat to high and bring the liquid to a boil. Skim off any impurities that rise to the surface. Lower the heat, cover, and simmer over low heat until the chickpeas are tender, approximately 1¼ hours. Season to taste with salt and pepper. Stir in the lemon juice to focus the flavors, adding a bit

more if necessary to achieve this effect.

The soup can be made to this point, and then cooled, covered, and refrigerated for up to 3 days. Reheat gently over low heat before proceeding.

Ladle the soup into individual warmed bowls, and garnish each serving with a scattering of cilantro.

PAIRING

Chicken Breasts Marinated with Lemon, Sage, and Aged Balsamic Vinegar (page 163)

FLAVOR BUILDING

Serve this over a hefty spoonful of Israeli couscous.

RICH SHORT RIB SOUP

Everyone thinks of short ribs as fodder for braising, but their intense flavor can be put to use in other ways, as it is in this recipe, which builds a soup around them. The ribs are browned and slowly simmered in stock until they are tender, then shredded and returned along with carrots, potatoes, and other vegetables, resulting in a dish brimming with potent flavors. SERVES 6

4 pounds beef short ribs, trimmed of excess fat and cut into 8 pieces

Coarse salt

Freshly ground black pepper

1 tablespoon olive oil

1 medium onion, peeled and halved

6 garlic cloves, crushed with the side of a knife and peeled

2 quarts Chicken Stock (page 31) or cold water

1 bouquet garni (2 bay leaves, 5 parsley sprigs, and 2 thyme sprigs, wrapped in the green top from a leek, below, and tied with kitchen string)

¾ cup diced carrots (large dice)

1½ cups diced Idaho potato

¾ cup diced celery (large dice)

½ cup sliced leeks, white part only (from about 2 medium leeks), well rinsed

Cracked black pepper, optional

Fleur de sel, optional

Thirty minutes before you plan to begin cooking, remove the short ribs from the refrigerator and season them generously with salt and pepper. Set them aside at room temperature.

Warm the oil in a large, heavy-bottomed pot set over medium heat. Add the meat and lightly brown it on all sides, about 3 minutes per side. (Tongs are a good tool for turning the ribs.) Transfer the ribs to a plate and set aside.

Add the onion to the pot, and cook for 4 minutes. Then add the garlic and cook for 1 minute. Add 1 cup of the stock. Scrape the bottom of the pot with a wooden spoon to loosen any flavorful bits. Return the ribs to the pot, and add the bouquet garni and the remaining stock. Raise the heat to medium-high and slowly bring the liquid to a boil. Skim off any impurities that rise to the surface. Reduce the heat, cover, and simmer, periodically skimming off any fat that rises to the surface, until the meat is fork-tender and falling off the bone, 2½ to 3 hours. Remove the pot from the heat.

Use a slotted spoon to remove the meat and bones from the pot, and set the meat aside to cool slightly. (Discard the bones.) As soon as the meat is cool enough to handle, trim off any remaining fat and shred the beef into large chunks.

Strain the broth through a fine-mesh sieve set over a bowl, and discard the solids. You should have approximately 4½ cups of liquid. Spoon off any fat that rises to the surface. Return the liquid to the pot, set the pot over medium-high heat, and cook for 6 to 8 minutes or until the liquid is reduced by one quarter, to concentrate the flavors. Add the carrots, potatoes, and celery, and cook until the vegetables are tender, about 12 minutes. Add the leeks and cook for 6 more minutes.

Return the meat to the pot and season the soup with salt and pepper.

The soup can be made to this point, then cooled, covered, and refrigerated for up to 3 days. Reheat gently over low heat before proceeding.

To serve, ladle the soup into individual warmed bowls and season with some cracked black pepper or a few grinds of black pepper from the mill. Pass fleur de sel alongside in a small bowl, if desired.

FLAVOR BUILDING

This soup can accommodate a wide variety of vegetables, including diced turnips, parsnips, celery root, cooked white beans (ideally Great Northern), and cooked savory cabbage. It's also a great vehicle for cooked cheese tortellini.

GRILLED VEGETABLE, ARUGULA, AND FRESH MOZZARELLA SANDWICH

When foods are marinated, it's usually done before they're cooked, but the vegetables in this sandwich are marinated after they've been grilled, when they've been softened up and can absorb the flavors better.

This recipe calls for Japanese eggplant, a beautiful, slender, lavender-colored relative of the American and European vegetable that, because it is less bitter, doesn't require salting. If you can get only regular eggplant, select the heaviest of the batch; more heft indicates fewer seeds and more edible flesh. To draw out the bitterness, salt the slices of regular eggplant and set them aside in a colander for half an hour before cooking.

Ideally, you should make this sandwich with *bufala mozzarella* from Italy because its creamy texture is without peer. A fresh American-made version will also be delicious. MAKES 4 SANDWICHES

---

2 large red bell peppers

1 large Japanese eggplant, cut on the diagonal into ¼-inch-thick slices

3 medium sweet onions (Maui, Vidalia, or red), each peeled and cut into 6 thick slices

¼ cup extra virgin olive oil, plus more for brushing the vegetables and bread

Coarse salt

Freshly ground black pepper

2 teaspoons red wine vinegar

1 garlic clove, peeled, halved, 1 half minced

1 teaspoon dried oregano

4 slices ciabatta or rosemary foccacia, cut ½ inch thick

8 ounces fresh mozzarella, cut into 8 slices

2 cups arugula leaves

5 leaves basil, cut into a chiffonade

Prepare an outdoor grill, letting the coals burn until they are covered with white ash. Roast the peppers on the grill until they are evenly charred all over, about 8 minutes. Put the peppers in a bowl, cover with plastic wrap, and let them steam in their own heat for 20 minutes.

Meanwhile, brush the eggplant and onion slices with olive oil, and season them with salt and pepper. Grill the slices on one side until nicely charred and smoky, approximately 3 minutes. Turn them and grill for another 2 minutes. Transfer the slices to a large platter and set aside.

By now, the peppers should be ready to be peeled. Remove them from the bowl and remove their skins with a paring knife; they should come right off. Stem and seed the peppers, and cut them lengthwise into wide strips. Add them to the platter with the onions and eggplant.

In a small bowl, whisk together the vinegar, minced garlic, oregano, and ¼ cup olive oil. Season the dressing with salt and pepper, pour it over the grilled vegetables, and let them marinate at room temperature for 30 minutes.

Meanwhile, brush the bread slices with olive oil, and season them with salt and pepper. Grill the bread until nicely toasted on both sides. Rub each slice with the cut clove of garlic.

To serve, place a slice of warm bread on each of four plates and top each slice with 2 slices of mozzarella. Arrange the vegetables on top of the cheese, along with some arugula leaves. There will be a few tablespoons of marinade remaining in the bowl; drizzle it over the sandwiches. Garnish each sandwich with basil chiffonade.

VARIATIONS

Feel free to grill your own favorite summer vegetables, such as yellow squash, green zucchini, leeks, tomatoes, mushrooms, and/or asparagus, for this sandwich.

Instead of garnishing with fresh basil, spread some Basil Pesto (page 110) on the bread before topping it with the vegetables.

ROAST TURKEY, AVOCADO, BACON, AND BLUE CHEESE SANDWICH

This sandwich borrows the signature combination of a Cobb salad, substituting turkey for the usual chicken. I've included it in this book as an excuse to share a recipe for brined turkey that we use quite a bit at home: rather than buy processed turkey, we purchase half a breast and brine it. This technique, which submerges the breast in a salted liquid with aromatics, is usually used before smoking to infuse meats with flavor and keep them juicy. Here, brining keeps the meat from drying out in the oven and extends its shelf life in the refrigerator. Once roasted, the turkey breast will provide you with the basis for two or three days' worth of sandwiches and salads.

This recipe also offers you the option of making the sandwich with aïoli, a versatile condiment that's also well worth adding to your repertoire. MAKES 4 SANDWICHES

1 turkey breast (3 pounds)

Turkey Breast Brine (recipe follows)

Freshly ground black pepper

2 tablespoons canola oil

8 ounces thickly sliced slab bacon

¼ cup Mayonnaise (page 51) or Aïoli (recipe follows)

8 thick slices ciabatta or Tuscan bread, lightly toasted or grilled

2 ripe avocados, halved, pitted, peeled, and thinly sliced

⅓ pound Maytag or Danish blue cheese

Tender inner romaine lettuce leaves

Coarse salt

Put the turkey breast in a nonreactive container and pour in the brine to completely cover it. Cover with plastic wrap and place in the refrigerator for 2 to 3 days. Remove the breast from the brine and pat it dry with paper towels. Season with pepper. Discard the brine.

Preheat the oven to 450°F.

Heat the oil in a small roasting pan set over high heat, and add the breast, skin side down. Place the pan in the oven and roast the turkey for 20 to 25 minutes, turning it over when the skin is nicely browned. Reduce the oven temperature to 325°F and cook until an instant-read thermometer inserted in the center of the breast reads 155°F, about 40 minutes more. Remove the pan from the oven and transfer the turkey to a cutting board to cool. Pour off any tasty bits of turkey from the roasting pan (they can be stirred into the mayonnaise for added flavor).

Cook the bacon in a sauté pan set over medium heat to your preferred degree of crispness.

Remove the breastbone from the turkey, and using a good knife, carve the turkey into enough thick slices for 4 sandwiches. (Leftovers can be used another day.)

To serve, build sandwiches in the usual way, spreading mayonnaise on the bread and adding the turkey, bacon, avocado, blue cheese, and lettuce. Season well with salt and pepper before placing the top slice of bread on each sandwich.

TURKEY BREAST BRINE

MAKES 2 QUARTS

2 quarts water

3 tablespoons sugar

3 tablespoons fine sea salt

2 bay leaves

2 tablespoons crushed juniper berries

Put all the ingredients in a medium saucepan set over high heat, and bring to a boil. Reduce the heat and simmer for 5 minutes. Cover the pot, remove it from the heat, and let cool at room temperature for 30 minutes. Chill the brine well in the refrigerator before using.

AÏOLI

This garlic mayonnaise can be used in endless ways—as a sauce for cooked vegetables, a sandwich spread, or an accompaniment to fish and shellfish.
MAKES 1 CUP

1 egg yolk, at room temperature

1½ tablespoons champagne vinegar, plus more if needed

1 teaspoon minced garlic, mashed with ¼ teaspoon coarse salt

Pinch of cayenne pepper

1 teaspoon finely chopped lemon zest

½ cup canola oil

¼ cup extra virgin olive oil

Coarse salt

Freshly ground white pepper to taste

In a small bowl, whisk together the egg yolk, vinegar, garlic, cayenne, and lemon zest. Whisk in some canola oil, a few drops at a time at first, then gradually in a very thin stream, to form a thick, emulsified mixture. Then whisk in the olive oil in the same way. Season to taste with salt and pepper. Use immediately, or cover and refrigerate for up to 3 days.

TURKEY BURGER

This turkey burger packs more flavor, has a more pleasing texture, and holds together better when cooked than others you might have had. To pull this off, I borrowed a trick from my mother. When she makes meatballs, she soaks bread cubes in half-and-half, then mixes them into the meat. Here this technique acts as a substitute for the fat in a beef burger, serving to keep the turkey burger soft and juicy. Juniper berries, thyme, garlic, and shallots give the turkey a much-needed jolt of flavor.

Serve the burgers on your favorite rolls, topped with traditional burger garnishes such as mayonnaise, onion, and tomato. SERVES 4

2 cups diced day-old bread (crusts removed, ½-inch dice)

½ cup half-and-half

1 pound ground turkey

1 large egg, beaten

1 tablespoon plus 1 teaspoon minced shallots

¼ teaspoon minced garlic

2 teaspoons chopped flat-leaf parsley

¼ teaspoon thyme leaves

½ teaspoon ground dried juniper berries

¼ teaspoon freshly ground black pepper

1 teaspoon coarse salt

2 tablespoons olive oil, plus more if needed

8 ounces Fontina or aged Gouda cheese, cut into 4 slices

4 hamburger rolls

Put the bread in a bowl and pour the half-and-half over it. Toss, and let soak until the bread has absorbed the liquid, approximately 20 minutes.

In a medium mixing bowl, combine the meat, egg, shallots, garlic, parsley, and thyme. Stir. Add the juniper berries, pepper, and salt. Add the soaked bread and mix to combine, using a rubber spatula or a wooden spoon. Wet your hands and divide the mixture into 4 patties. Set the patties on a plate lined with plastic wrap (to prevent sticking). Better yet, set them on individual squares of wax or parchment paper.

Preheat the broiler.

You may need to do the following in batches: Heat the olive oil in a nonstick sauté pan set over medium heat. Add the patties and cook for 6 minutes per side, turning them carefully with a slotted spatula. Add more oil between batches if necessary.

Place the burgers on a cookie sheet, top with the cheese, and heat under the broiler until the cheese softens and begins to melt, about 2 minutes. Serve immediately in the hamburger rolls.

GRILLED PIZZA WITH POTATOES, CARMELIZED ONIONS, AND RACLETTE

This pizza takes its cue from a French and Swiss tradition that involves melting a piece of raclette—a Swiss cow's-milk cheese—and serving it with accompaniments like potatoes, onions, and bread. If it sounds like fondue on a plate, that's about right. This is a highly romanticized dish; there are machines designed expressly to cook the cheese, and the ritual of eating it is often associated with ski vacations when it might be prepared right in the fireplace.

Raclette, the dish, and raclette, the cheese, are inseparable (the name actually means "to scrape"), though the cheese can be served as part of a traditional cheese plate. MAKES 4 INDIVIDUAL PIZZAS

Coarse salt

5 small Yukon Gold potatoes

2 or 3 large garlic cloves, unpeeled

About ¼ cup extra virgin olive oil

Freshly ground black pepper

2 small onions, peeled and thinly sliced (about 3 cups sliced)

1 tablespoon sugar

2 tablespoons balsamic vinegar

All-purpose flour, for dusting the work surface

1¼ pounds raw pizza dough, divided into 4 balls

2 cups grated Swiss raclette cheese (6 to 8 ounces)

1 tablespoon chopped rosemary

Bring a pot of lightly salted water to a boil. Add the potatoes and garlic, and cook for 35 minutes. Drain, reserving the garlic. While they are still warm, peel the potatoes and slice them into thin rounds. Drizzle with 2 tablespoons of the oil, and season to taste with salt and pepper. Set aside.

Squeeze the cooked garlic into a small bowl and mash it to a paste with 1 tablespoon of the oil. Season with salt and pepper, and set aside.

Lightly oil a sauté pan set over medium-high heat. Add the onions, season with salt and pepper, and sauté for 5 minutes. Add the sugar, lower the heat to medium, and cook, stirring often, until the onions are soft and nicely caramelized, approximately 20 minutes. Add the vinegar and cook until reduced to a glaze, about 2 minutes. Taste, and adjust the seasoning if necessary. Remove the pan from the heat and set it aside.

Preheat the oven to 450°F. Prepare an outdoor grill, letting the coals burn until they are covered with white ash.

Dust a board or work surface with the flour, and turn the balls of dough out onto it. One ball at a time, roll out the dough, working it to an even thickness of ¼ inch, shaping it into a free-form rectangle, leaving it a bit rough around the edges for a rustic appearance. Lightly oil a cookie sheet, or two if necessary, and place the pizzas on it to bring them to the grill.

Brush the tops of the pizzas with olive oil and season them with salt and pepper. Place the pizzas on the grill without crowding. Cook for about 1 minute, rotating them a quarter-turn every 15 or 20 seconds to ensure they cook evenly. Use the tongs to carefully turn the pizzas over, and cook them on the other side, rotating them again.

The pizzas can be made to this point and held at room temperature for up to 1 hour.

Return the pizzas to the cookie sheet(s) and brush them with the garlic paste. Arrange the raclette, potatoes, and onions on the pizzas, and sprinkle them with the rosemary. Season with salt and pepper. Bake the pizzas, two at a time, in the oven until the cheese melts, about 5 minutes.

Remove the pizzas from the oven, cut them into pieces with a large knife or a pizza cutter, and serve at once.

GRILLED PIZZA WITH TOMATO, RICOTTA, PROSCIUTTO, AND ARUGULA

The most traditional pizza in the book, this one features some of my favorite Italian ingredients: a simple homemade tomato sauce; cool, creamy ricotta cheese; silky, salty prosciutto; and peppery arugula. I developed the sauce—more of a paste really—to ensure a crisp crust. As with any recipe this simple, the quality of the ingredients is paramount here, so substitute as necessary to ensure that only the very best is used. This would also be delicious made with mozzarella and grated Parmigiano-Reggiano, thin slices of soppressata or Tuscan salami, and/or sautéed mushrooms. MAKES 4 INDIVIDUAL PIZZAS

All-purpose flour, for dusting the work surface

1¼ pounds raw pizza dough, divided into 4 balls

¼ cup extra virgin olive oil

Coarse salt

Freshly ground black pepper

1 cup Pizza Sauce (recipe follows)

1½ cups fresh ricotta cheese

¼ pound Parmigiano-Reggiano, grated with a microplane grater or on the smallest holes of a box grater

⅓ pound thinly sliced prosciutto di Parma (about 12 thin slices)

2 bunches arugula, stems removed (about 2 cups leaves)

6 leaves basil, cut into a chiffonade

Preheat the oven to 425°F. Prepare an outdoor grill, letting the coals burn until they are covered with white ash.

Dust a board or work surface with the flour and turn the balls of dough out onto it. One ball at a time, roll out the dough, working it to an even thickness of ¼ inch, shaping it into a free-form rectangle, leaving it a bit rough around the edges for a rustic appearance. Lightly oil a cookie sheet, or two if necessary, and place the pizzas on it to bring them to the grill.

Brush the tops of the pizzas with olive oil and season them with salt and pepper. Place the pizzas on the grill without crowding. Cook for about 1 minute, rotating them a quarter-turn every 15 or 20 seconds to ensure they cook evenly. Use the tongs to carefully turn the pizzas over, and cook them on the other side, rotating them again.

The pizzas can be made to this point and held at room temperature for up to 1 hour.

Return the pizzas to the cookie sheet(s) and spread the Pizza Sauce lightly over the surfaces. Distribute spoonfuls of ricotta around the surface of the pizzas, and scatter the Parmesan cheese over the top. Bake in the oven for 3 minutes.

Remove the sheet(s) from the oven and arrange the prosciutto slices and arugula attractively over the pizzas. Drizzle with olive oil, top with the basil, season with salt and pepper, and serve at once.

PIZZA SAUCE

Bocce's Pizza in Buffalo, New York, is my personal pizza touchstone. Their sauce is the one I grew up on and the one I aim to replicate. Tomato paste is the key, with plenty of extra virgin olive oil, garlic, oregano, and other traditional ingredients added for something that I hope will trigger your best pizza memories, too. MAKES 1 CUP

⅔ cup tomato paste

2 tablespoons extra virgin olive oil

2 teaspoons finely chopped rinsed anchovy fillets (from about 3 fillets)

½ teaspoon finely chopped garlic, mashed with a pinch of salt

½ teaspoon dried oregano

¼ teaspoon freshly ground black pepper

¼ teaspoon crushed red pepper flakes

½ teaspoon coarse salt

In a medium, stainless steel mixing bowl, combine all of the ingredients, ideally stirring them together with a small rubber spatula.

PIZZA WITH ROASTED CHILES, MANCHEGO, AND SCALLIONS

This intensely spicy pizza uses smoky adobo sauce in place of tomato sauce and calls for a number of chile peppers to be scattered over the pie. I encourage you to select a variety of peppers, not just for the varying levels of sweetness and spice, but also for the spectrum of colors. At its best, this pizza will be a kaleidoscope of heat, one that would be perfectly complemented by an ice-cold beer.

If your palate is sensitive to heat, use sweet peppers instead of hot ones; this will still be delicious.

MAKES 4 INDIVIDUAL PIZZAS

16 assorted small fresh chile peppers (jalapeño, serrano, Anaheim, red Italian, Fresno, cherry) and the chipotle from the can of adobo

3 tablespoons olive oil, plus more for brushing the cookie sheet and the pizzas

1 teaspoon freshly squeezed lemon juice

1 garlic clove, halved lengthwise, 1 half minced

Coarse salt

Freshly ground black pepper

All-purpose flour, for dusting the work surface

1¼ pounds raw pizza dough, divided into 4 balls

¼ cup adobo sauce (from 1 can chipotle peppers in adobo sauce)

1 pound Manchego, Monterey Jack, Istara, or Pyrenees cheese, grated (about 4 cups grated)

8 scallions, white and light green parts only, thinly sliced

¼ cup coarsely chopped cilantro leaves

Prepare an outdoor grill, letting the coals burn until they are covered with white ash. Preheat the oven to 450°F.

Holding them with a long set of tongs or a meat fork, roast the peppers over an open flame or on the grill until they are charred and smoky all over, about 7 minutes. Put them in a bowl, cover with plastic wrap, and let them steam in their own heat for 15 minutes. Wearing rubber gloves to protect your hands, remove the peppers from the bowl and peel them; their skins should come right off with the aid of a paring knife. Seed and slice or dice them, and set them aside.

Pour the olive oil into a bowl. Add the lemon juice and minced garlic, and season with salt and pepper. Pour this mixture over the peppers and let them marinate while you make the pizzas.

Dust a board or work surface with flour and turn the balls of dough out onto it. One ball at a time, roll out the dough, working it to an even thickness of ¼ inch, shaping it into a free-form rectangle, leaving

it a bit rough around the edges for a rustic appearance. Lightly oil a cookie sheet, or two if necessary, and place the pizzas on it to bring them to the grill.

Brush the tops of the pizzas with olive oil, and season them with salt and pepper. Place the pizzas on the grill without crowding. Cook for about 1 minute, rotating them a quarter-turn every 15 or 20 seconds to ensure they cook evenly. Use the tongs to carefully turn the pizzas over, and cook them on the other side, rotating them again.

The pizzas can be made to this point and held at room temperature for up to 1 hour.

Return the pizzas to the cookie sheet(s), rub them with the half clove of garlic, and brush the adobo sauce over them. Sprinkle with the cheese and peppers. Bake them, two at a time, in the oven until the cheese melts, about 5 minutes.

Remove the pizzas from the oven, garnish with the scallions and cilantro, and cut them into pieces with a large knife or a pizza cutter. Serve at once.

PASTA AND RISOTTO

WHEN IT COMES TO PASTA AND RISOTTO, I'M AN UNABASHED
purist. Though I create original dishes, I do so using exclusively Italian, or at least Mediterranean, ingredients. Maybe it's because of my Italian heritage, but when I think of pasta and risotto, I think of tomatoes, prosciutto di Parma, fresh shellfish, preserved tuna, sausage, and, of course, extra virgin olive oil
and grated Italian cheeses. The list is finite, but the possibilities it presents are virtually limitless.

I must admit to one small exception: Farfalle with Smoked Salmon, Snow Peas, and a Lemon-Herb
Vinaigrette, a cold pasta salad, is a distinctly American invention.

PASTA

The simplicity of the following recipes illustrates an important point: Pasta lends itself to innumerable
options beyond the all-too-familiar cream sauces and long-simmered red sauces. In many of the dishes
one or two ingredients emulsify just enough to unite the others and coat the pasta, making a separately
cooked sauce unnecessary.

When you do opt for a sauce, these recipes show you ways of making something a little different,
like Spaghetti with Hot and Sweet Peppers, which skips the stalwarts of tomatoes and cream, instead
fashioning a light sauté of peppers, onions, garlic, and stock. Even a dish like Fresh Linguine with Heirloom Tomatoes, Ricotta Salata, and Basil Pesto offers an approach that will be new to many: an uncooked
tomato mixture is tossed with the hot pasta, which warms it just enough to unlock and integrate the
flavors.

Sometimes home cooks find themselves in a quandary as to what pasta shape to choose for a particular dish. Of course it's not prudent to have too-rigid a rule because every recipe should be considered on its own terms, but I offer the following general guidelines: Relatively rich or creamy sauces, especially those made with braised meats, usually demand a substantial pasta that won't be overwhelmed, such as pappardelle or rigatoni. Long, thin pasta strands, on the other hand, tend to be more suitable to lighter sauces, like those based on summer vegetables and seafood. Smaller dried pasta shapes, such as penne and orecchiette, work best when there are several distinct components in the bowl and you want each bite to capture bits of all of them.

RISOTTO

Risotto has a reputation for being difficult to make, but in reality is much simpler and more forgiving than many pasta dishes. The basic procedure is to make the risotto itself, then stir in the other ingredients, which have been cooked separately, at the last second. Generally speaking, the crucial requirements for a successful risotto are rather abstract: risotto-making calls for patience and attention because the rice must be stirred slowly over a period of about 20 minutes, and each ladleful of stock should be added only after the last addition as been absorbed.

The most important tangible ingredients are a *superfino* (medium-grain) rice such as Arborio, Canaroli, or Vialone Nano, and a high-quality stock. As they slowly cook in the stock, these rice varieties release their starch, which is what binds the individual grains together. And because the rice itself is the dominant ingredient in any risotto dish, the stock it absorbs—its source of flavor—should be home-made, or at least one of the premium organic brands now available in most supermarkets.

I also appreciate risotto's versatility. Like pasta, it can be served as a first or a main course and, on occasion, as an accompaniment.

Another aspect of risotto that is so charmingly utilitarian and often overlooked is that it's one of the best ways to avail yourself of on-hand ingredients by making them the centerpiece of an improvised dish that requires little else beyond rice and stock. It's not an oversimplification to say that once you've made a few risotto recipes, you will be well equipped to create your own by following these examples. Select the appropriate stock for what you have in mind, prepare the ingredients to be added at the end, and make the risotto itself following the basic instructions included in each of the following recipes.

I find risotto to be a very user-friendly dish for entertaining because—contrary to popular belief—it can be made in advance, which is essential when hosting guests. Here's how you do it:

Make the risotto according to the recipe instructions, stopping just before adding the second-to-last ladleful of stock. (There should be a cup or two of simmering stock left.) Turn the risotto out on a cookie sheet lined with parchment paper, spreading it out evenly to let it cool as quickly as possible. When it is cool, immediately spoon the risotto into an airtight container and seal it, to make sure the rice doesn't absorb any additional moisture. It can be kept in this container at room temperature for up to 2 hours. When you are ready to serve it, return the rice to a hot pot and stir in the final addition or two of stock. Warm or re-warm the ingredients you'll be adding to the risotto, then stir them in, cooking for 5 minutes.

FRESH LINGUINE WITH HEIRLOOM TOMATOES, RICOTTA SALATA, AND BASIL PESTO

This flexible recipe accommodates any variety of tomatoes; in fact, it's best with a mix of the full spectrum from pale yellow to bright red. The tomatoes' flavor is perked up first by marinating and then by contact with the hot pasta, which also unlocks the full aromatic power of the basil. It's no exaggeration to say that this dish will smell of the season when it arrives at the table.

Often, either Parmigiano or pecorino will do just fine as a grating cheese for pasta dishes. This recipe, however, also calls for ricotta salata, a gently salted sheep's-milk cheese. Try to find one from Sicily, where it was first produced, that has been aged for at least one year. This ricotta salata is harder than the rest and is intended specifically for grating. SERVES 6 AS AN APPETIZER OR 4 AS A MAIN COURSE

2½ pounds heirloom tomatoes, a multicolored mix of yellow, orange, red, green, and/or purple

½ teaspoon minced garlic

¼ cup plus 2 tablespoons extra virgin olive oil, plus more for serving

2 tablespoons minced shallots

1 teaspoon aged red wine vinegar

1 teaspoon balsamic vinegar

Coarse salt

Freshly ground black pepper

12 ounces fresh linguine

4 ounces aged ricotta salata, coarsely grated

1 tablespoon chopped flat-leaf parsley

¼ cup grated Parmigiano-Reggiano

2 tablespoons Basil Pesto (recipe follows) or basil chiffonade

Bring a large pot of water to a boil and fill a large bowl halfway with ice water. Remove the tomatoes' stems, cutting out a small circle of skin around them. Cut a small, shallow X on the bottom of each tomato, just deep enough to puncture the skin. Lower the tomatoes into the boiling water for 10 to 20 seconds, depending on their ripeness. (The riper the tomato, the less time is required.) Use tongs or a slotted spoon to transfer the tomatoes to the ice water. As the tomatoes cool, the skin will begin to pull away from the flesh. Peel the tomatoes (the skin should come right off with the aid of a paring knife), halve them crosswise, and squeeze out the seeds. Cut the flesh into large dice and set aside.

In a bowl that is large enough to hold all of the ingredients, gather the tomatoes, garlic, olive oil, shallots, and both vinegars. Toss, and season to taste with salt and pepper. Let marinate at room temperature for 30 minutes to 1 hour.

Bring a large pot of salted water to a boil. Add the pasta and cook for 2 to 3 minutes. While the pasta is cooking, taste the tomatoes and adjust the seasoning if necessary. Drain the pasta, add it to the tomatoes, and toss to combine.

Use tongs to serve the pasta from the bowl, topping each serving with a good mix of tomatoes, then finishing it with some ricotta salata, parsley, Parmigiano, and a dollop of pesto.

PAIRING

Fig, Prosciutto, and Arugula Salad with Goat Cheese and a Balsamic-Honey Drizzle (page 43)

VARIATIONS

This pasta is equally delicious cold, which makes it an ideal dish for late-summer picnics.

The shaved ricotta salata can be replaced with crumbled fresh goat cheese or Roquefort.

BASIL PESTO

Years ago, on a vacation in Italy's Cinque Terre, Helen and I discovered the wonder of pesto made in the region where it was invented, as the ultimate expression of the flavor of the delicate little Genovese basil leaves that grow in Liguria. It's difficult to find these perfect leaves here in the United States, but Helen has spent years tinkering with her pesto recipe to approximate the light, fluffy quality of the one we sampled there.

We've always described the basil pesto we had in Italy as resembling pale green whipped cream. Helen has finally acted on that visual cue, adding heavy cream (and fresh bread crumbs) to the basil, parmesan cheese, and pine nuts. This produces a beautiful, bright green sauce that is full of flavor yet delicate, especially if you use small young leaves, which you can often find in late August; larger leaves have a harsher flavor. Blanching the leaves, an unusual step in pesto-making, further softens their flavor.

This pesto will hold perfectly for a few hours at room temperature and is at its best if served within that time, though it can be covered and refrigerated for a few days.

Just as a sharp blade makes a difference when using a knife, a sharp processor blade will prevent the basil from bruising and will result in a much finer texture here.

This pesto has many applications, but I enjoy it especially when it is smeared on thick slices of tomato or stirred into mayonnaise. MAKES 1½ CUPS

⅓ cup fresh bread crumbs

2 tablespoons heavy cream

2 cups (packed) basil leaves

1 large garlic clove, peeled and minced

About ½ cup extra virgin olive oil

½ cup pine nuts, ground in a food processor or with a mortar and pestle

½ cup grated Parmigiano-Reggiano

Pinch of cayenne pepper, optional

½ teaspoon coarse salt

Several grindings of black pepper

Bring a pot of salted water to a boil. Fill a bowl halfway with ice water. In a small bowl, moisten the bread crumbs with the cream.

Add the basil leaves to the boiling water and blanch for 15 seconds. Strain them, then plunge them into the ice water to stop the cooking and preserve their bright color.

Gently squeeze as much excess moisture as possible from the basil leaves and place them in the bowl of a food processor fitted with the metal blade. Add the garlic and ¼ cup of the olive oil. Process, adding some of the remaining oil if necessary, until the mixture is smooth and thick. Add the bread crumb–cream mixture, pine nuts, cheese, cayenne pepper, if using, salt, and black pepper. Process once again until smooth. Taste, and adjust the seasoning if necessary.

Transfer the pesto a small bowl, and if not serving it immediately, cover it with plastic wrap, laying the film directly on the surface of the pesto.

WHOLE WHEAT SPAGHETTI, SAUTÉED RADICCHIO, GARLIC, AND PARMIGIANO-REGGIANO

One of the most uncomplicated and delicious classic Tuscan pasta dishes goes as follows: Heat some olive oil in a sauté pan, add sliced garlic, and toss it with hot spaghetti. This dish uses that basic recipe with a few simple additions. Radicchio contributes a touch of bitterness and crunch, while whole wheat pasta provides an appealing nutty flavor. SERVES 4

½ cup extra virgin olive oil

2 garlic cloves, crushed with the side of a knife and peeled, plus 2 tablespoons thinly sliced garlic

Four ¼-inch-thick slices good-quality white bread, crusts removed, cut into small dice (about ½ cup diced)

½ teaspoon chopped thyme leaves

Coarse salt

Freshly ground black pepper

1 pound dried whole wheat spaghetti

1 medium head radicchio, cored, leaves stacked and thickly julienned

2 tablespoons chopped flat-leaf parsley

4 ounces Parmigiano-Reggiano, grated

Preheat the oven to 325°F.

Heat 2 tablespoons of the olive oil in an ovenproof sauté pan set over medium heat. Add the crushed garlic and sauté for 4 minutes. Add the bread cubes, thyme, and another 2 tablespoons of the olive oil. Season with salt and pepper, and stir. Transfer the pan to the oven and cook, stirring regularly, until the bread cubes are crisp all over, about 15 minutes. Remove the pan from the oven and let the croutons cool. Then crush them to make bread crumbs. Set aside.

Bring a large pot of salted water to a boil. Add the spaghetti and cook until al dente, about 8 minutes.

Meanwhile, heat 2 tablespoons of the oil in a large saucepan set over medium-high heat. Add the sliced garlic and cook until lightly browned for 3 minutes. Add the radicchio, season with salt and pepper, and cook until softened, 3 to 4 minutes.

Reserve ¼ cup of the pasta cooking liquid, then drain the pasta. Add the pasta, parsley, half the cheese, and a few grindings of black pepper to the pan containing the radicchio.

Slowly add the remaining 2 tablespoons oil, then the reserved pasta liquid, in a thin stream, tossing to create a light emulsion.

To serve, transfer the pasta to a warmed serving bowl, cover with a light dusting of the remaining cheese and the bread crumbs, and serve family-style from the center of the table.

PAIRING

Chicken Breasts Marinated with Lemon, Sage, and Aged Balsamic Vinegar (page 163)

VARIATION

The radicchio can be replaced by broccoli rabe or dandelion greens.

FLAVOR BUILDING

Tossing in 2 tablespoons unsalted butter along with the cheese at the end will enrich the dish, adding body to the sauce.

If they're in season, toss in 1 cup diced tomatoes at the end.

TAGLIATELLE WITH SQUID, SCALLOPS, AND SHRIMP

In this dish, anchovies, tomatoes, garlic, capers, red pepper flakes, parsley, and basil come together in a quick, un-cooked tomato sauce that's warmed when tossed with just-sautéed shellfish. As if this weren't easy enough, the sauce can be made hours, or a day, in advance and set aside in the refrigerator until you're ready to serve the pasta. Like so many pasta recipes, this one lends itself to interpretation and adaptation; the most successful variations focus on just one type of shellfish. Make your decision at the market: if the scallops seem superior to the shrimp, make them the center of the dish. SERVES 4

Coarse salt

1 tablespoon finely chopped, rinsed salt-packed anchovy fillets (from 8 to 10 fillets)

2 cups chopped canned whole tomatoes, drained

2 teaspoons tomato paste

1 teaspoon minced garlic, mashed with a pinch of coarse salt

4 teaspoons coarsely chopped rinsed capers

¾ teaspoon sugar

¼ teaspoon crushed red pepper flakes

3 tablespoons extra virgin olive oil

Freshly ground black pepper

8 ounces bay or small sea scallops

8 ounces large shrimp, peeled and deveined (about 12 shrimp)

8 ounces cleaned squid, sliced crosswise into thick rings

¼ cup dry white wine

12 ounces fresh tagliatelle pasta

¼ cup heavy cream

4 teaspoons unsalted butter

¼ cup chopped flat-leaf parsley

1 heaping tablespoon chopped basil leaves

Bring a pot of salted water to a boil.

Meanwhile, in a bowl, make the tomato sauce: Stir together the anchovies, tomatoes, tomato paste, garlic, capers, sugar, red pepper flakes, and 2 tablespoons of the olive oil. Season to taste with salt and pepper.

Heat the remaining 1 tablespoon oil in a wide, deep sauté pan set over medium heat. Season the scallops with salt and pepper, add them to the pan, and sauté until just seared and firm to the touch, approximately 2 minutes, depending on their thickness. Add the shrimp and sauté until firm and pink, approximately 2 minutes, depending on their size. Add the squid and cook until they just begin to turn opaque, approximately 1 minute. Add the white wine and deglaze the pan.

Pour in the tomato sauce and bring it to a simmer over medium-high heat, approximately 2 minutes. As the sauce warms, add the pasta to the boiling water and cook it for 2 to 3 minutes.

Once the sauce is simmering, stir in the cream. Remove the pan from the heat and stir in the butter, then the parsley and basil. Drain the pasta and add it to the pan. Toss, taste, and adjust the seasoning with salt and pepper if necessary.

To serve, transfer the pasta to a warmed bowl and present it family-style from the center of the table.

PAIRING

Filet Mignon with Madeira Sauce (page 178)

VARIATION

Another version of this pasta uses only squid; if you opt to do the same, deglaze with red wine instead of white.

FLAVOR BUILDING

Stir in some diced cooked lobster meat just before serving.

Steamed mussels in their shells would also be a logical addition. Arrange them decoratively atop the pasta in the serving bowl. Strain the steaming liquid, and stir some into the sauce.

Olives and saffron are age-old complements to shellfish: add ½ cup pitted Niçoise olives and/or a pinch of saffron while heating the sauce.

FETTUCCINE WITH PRESERVED TUNA, CAPERS, AND OLIVES

I grew up in a household where we didn't eat meat on Friday, which presented a problem because when I was a child, I didn't like most fish or shellfish. My mother solved this dilemma by making me pasta with canned tuna and tomato sauce. This is my adult version of that recipe, made with high-quality preserved tuna with capers and anchovies added to hit the notes one expects in such a classic seafood pasta. SERVES 4

Coarse salt

1 pound dried fettuccine

¼ cup extra virgin olive oil

2 teaspoons minced garlic

6 anchovy fillets, rinsed, dried, and minced

1½ cups canned tomato puree

1 tablespoon capers, rinsed and chopped

¼ cup Gaeta olives, pitted and chopped

14 ounces excellent-quality tuna preserved in olive oil, store-bought or homemade (page 60)

Freshly ground black pepper

2 tablespoons chopped flat-leaf parsley

Bring a pot of salted water to a boil. Add the pasta and cook just until al dente, about 7 minutes.

Meanwhile, heat the oil in a wide, deep sauté pan set over medium heat. Add the garlic and cook until golden-brown, about 2 minutes. Add the anchovies and cook for 2 minutes more. Stir in the tomato puree and capers.

Reserve ¼ cup of the cooking liquid, then strain the pasta. Stir the olives and tuna into the sauce, then gradually stir in the reserved pasta water until the sauce attains a pleasing consistency. Add the hot pasta and toss. Season with pepper and toss again.

To serve, divide the hot pasta among individual warmed bowls, topping each serving with some chopped parsley.

FLAVOR BUILDING
Add ½ teaspoon chopped fresh rosemary to the sauce along with the black pepper.

ORECCHIETTE WITH SHELL BEANS, PROSCIUTTO, AND PARMIGIANO-REGGIANO

Orecchiette, an ear-shaped pasta, has a pleasingly thick and chewy mouthfeel; it suggests a cross between pasta and gnocchi, particularly if the orecchiette is fresh. That is why it's most often served with broccoli rabe and hot sausage; its sturdy texture lets you taste the pasta itself, even alongside such assertive ingredients as bitter greens and spicy, ground pork. Orecchiette also has the appealing ability to absorb liquid better than most other pastas, a quality that is used to full effect in this version of *pasta en brodo*, or pasta in broth. The final cooking step gives the orecchiette a chance to swell up with as much flavor as possible just before serving. For this reason, use your best, richest home-made stock. SERVES 4

Coarse salt

½ cup fava beans, from about 1 pound beans in the pod, or 1 cup green and yellow wax beans cut into 1-inch pieces

1⅓ cups dried orecchiette pasta

¾ cup fresh sweet peas (defrosted frozen peas can be substituted)

¾ cup fresh cranberry beans (dried can be substituted; soak them overnight in enough cold water to cover by 1 inch, then drain)

1 tablespoon extra virgin olive oil plus 4 tablespoons for serving

1 piece prosciutto di Parma, 2 ounces, cut into ¼-inch dice

1 tablespoon minced shallots

1 teaspoon minced garlic

3 cups Chicken Stock (page 31)

1 heaping tablespoon basil chiffonade

½ cup finely grated Parmigiano-Reggiano cheese

Freshly ground black pepper to taste

Bring a pot of salted water to boil. Fill a large bowl halfway with ice water.

When the water boils, add the fava beans and cook for 4 minutes. (If using wax beans, cook for 2 to 3 minutes.) Remove with a slotted spoon or small strainer and shock them in the ice water to stop the cooking and preserve their color. Repeat with the peas, cooking for 2 to 3 minutes, then the cranberry beans, cooking for 6 minutes. Drain all the peas and beans and set aside.

Bring a large pot of salted water to a boil.

Meanwhile, pour the oil into a large pot set over medium heat. Add the prosciutto and cook, stirring, until lightly browned, about 4 minutes. Add the shallots and cook until softened but not browned, 2 minutes. Add the garlic and cook for 1 minute more. Pour in the stock, raise the heat to high, bring to a boil until reduced to 1½ cups, approximately 10 minutes to concentrate the flavors.

Add the orecchiette to the boiling water and cook until just al dente, 8 to 10 minutes. Drain the pasta and toss it with a few drops of olive oil to prevent the pasta from sticking. Set it aside.

Once the sauce has reduced, taste and adjust the seasoning with salt and pepper if necessary. Lower the heat and add the beans, pasta, basil, and a few tablespoons of grated cheese, and cook until the beans are warmed through and the pasta has absorbed some of the sauce, about 2 minutes.

To serve, divide the pasta among individual bowls, topping each serving with some grated cheese and a drizzle of oil.

PAIRINGS

Roasted Halibut with Lemon-Caper Butter (page 155), Lime and Butter-Braised Fluke (page 152)

VARIATIONS

The foundation of pasta, stock, and prosciutto will support almost any combination of spring or summer beans and vegetables. Use a combination of dried and fresh beans or add asparagus tips and chopped broccoli.

Pancetta or bacon can replace the prosciutto.

FLAVOR BUILDING

Put a spoonful of Basil Pesto (page 110) in the center of each bowl.

PAPPARDELLE WITH BRAISED LAMB SHANK AND FONTINA

In Italian households, a popular way of using leftover braised meats is to chop or shred the meat, return it to its own sauce, and toss it with fresh pasta. This recipe goes right to the pasta stage, using the intensely vinous braising liquid as a sauce. Don't be too casual with your choice of Fontina cheeses: Though produced in many countries, including the United States, the best is Fontina d'Aosta, which comes from the Piedmont region of northern Italy. Its fresh flavor makes a big impact on the overall success of this dish. The pappardelle, probably most often seen with rabbit on restaurant menus, is the perfect choice for lamb shanks and other braised-meat sauces.

If you can find it, replace the Parmigiano-Reggiano with an aged Pepato, a Sicilian pecorino punctuated with whole black peppercorns. When the cheese is shaved, the flavor of the pepper is unleashed as well, adding a whole new meaning to the term "freshly grated black pepper." SERVES 6 AS AN APPETIZER OR 4 AS A MAIN COURSE

2 tablespoons canola oil

2 lamb shanks (1½ pounds each)

Coarse salt

Freshly ground black pepper

½ cup diced onion

2 garlic cloves, peeled and thinly sliced

¼ cup diced celery

¼ cup diced carrot

2½ cups robust Italian red wine

1 cup canned tomato puree

1 tablespoon tomato paste

1 thyme sprig

1 rosemary sprig

1 bay leaf

1 quart Chicken Stock (page 31), or more as needed

1 pound fresh pappardelle pasta

8 ounces Fontina cheese, coarsely grated

¼ cup chopped flat-leaf parsley

½ cup basil chiffonade

Preheat the oven to 300°F.

Pour the oil into a heavy-bottomed ovenproof pot that is just large enough to hold the lamb shanks, and set the pot over medium-high heat. Season the lamb shanks with salt and pepper, add them to the pot, and cook, turning often, until nicely browned all over, approximately 10 minutes. Remove the shanks from the pot and set them aside.

Add the onions, garlic, celery, and carrots to the pot and sauté until softened but not browned, approximately 5 minutes. Add the wine, raise the heat to high, bring it to a boil, and continue to boil until reduced to ¼ cup, approximately 12 minutes. Stir in the tomato puree, tomato paste, thyme, rosemary, and bay leaf, and cook for 6 more minutes. Add the 1 quart stock and bring it to a simmer.

Return the shanks to the pot. If the liquid doesn't completely cover them, add some more stock. When the liquid returns to a simmer, cover the pot with foil or a tight-fitting lid, place it in the oven, and braise the shanks for 2½ hours. Check periodically to be sure the liquid is just barely simmering. If it's bubbling aggressively, lower the temperature by 25 degrees. After the 2½ hours, the meat should pull away from the bone with just the tug of a fork; if it offers any resistance, continue to cook for 15 more minutes. When the shanks are done, remove the pot from the oven, remove the foil, and remove the shanks from the pot, setting them on a cutting board. Set the pot aside to let the liquid cool for about 15 minutes. When the shanks are cool enough to handle, remove the meat from the bones, and chop or shred it.

Use tongs to remove and discard the bay leaf, thyme, and rosemary from the braising liquid; discard them. Skim off any fat that has risen to the surface. Then place the pot over high heat, bring the liquid to a boil, and let it boil, skimming off any impurities that rise to the surface, until reduced to 2 cups, about 30 minutes.

Meanwhile, bring a large pot of salted water to a boil over high heat. Add the pasta and cook for 2 to 3 minutes.

Drain the pasta and transfer it to a large warmed bowl. Add the reserved meat, the sauce, and the cheese, parsley, and basil. Toss, season with salt and pepper, then divide among individual plates or bowls and serve at once.

VARIATIONS

This dish would also be delicious made with veal shanks (2 inches thick and cooked for 2 hours), or duck or rabbit legs (cooked for 1 to 1½ hours).

Rigatoni has the size and thickness to stand up to such a rich sauce, so use it in place of pappardelle if you like.

FLAVOR BUILDING

Top each serving with a creamy dollop of fresh ricotta for a stark yet sublime contrast of flavor and color.

FARFALLE WITH SMOKED SALMON, SNOW PEAS, AND A LEMON-HERB VINAIGRETTE

Although they're very popular in the United States, cold pasta dishes are rarely found in Italy. Like most American pasta salads, this one has a mayonnaise dressing, but the proportions of the ingredients result in a bright, lemony, herbaceous dressing that's not unctuous or overwhelming. The recipe calls for mixed herbs, but you can focus on just one if you like; dill would be the most logical candidate because of its natural affinity with salmon. SERVES 4 TO 6

Coarse salt

4 ounces snow peas

1 large egg yolk, at room temperature

2 tablespoons freshly squeezed lemon juice, plus more to finish, plus 1 teaspoon finely grated lemon zest

1 teaspoon Dijon mustard

¼ teaspoon minced garlic

⅛ teaspoon cayenne pepper

1 cup plus 2 tablespoons extra virgin olive oil

½ cup grapeseed or canola oil

Freshly ground black pepper to taste

1 pound dried farfalle (bow-tie) pasta

1 cup watercress leaves or pea greens

¼ cup thinly sliced scallions, white part plus 1 inch of green

8 ounces smoked salmon, cut into wide ribbons

¼ cup mixed fresh herb leaves, such as chives, dill, tarragon, and chervil

Bring a pot of lightly salted water to a boil over high heat. Fill a large bowl halfway with ice water. Add the snow peas to the boiling water and cook them until just tender, approximately 1 minute. Use a slotted spoon to transfer them to the ice water to stop the cooking and preserve their color.

Drain them, julienne them, and set them aside.

In a bowl, whisk together the egg yolk, 1 tablespoon of the lemon juice, the mustard, garlic, cayenne, and a pinch of salt, either by hand or using an electric mixer. Add the 1 cup olive oil, a drop at a time at first, and then in a thin steady stream, whisking constantly to form an emulsified dressing. Whisk in the lemon zest, the remaining 1 tablespoon lemon juice, and the grapeseed oil. If the dressing is too thick, whisk in a few drops of warm water. Season to taste with salt and pepper and set it aside.

Bring a pot of salted water to a boil. Add the pasta and cook until al dente, 8 to 9 minutes. Drain the pasta and transfer it to a bowl.

Add the watercress to the bowl, along with the remaining 2 tablespoons olive oil. Toss, then let cool at room temperature for 10 minutes. Add the snow peas, scallions, salmon, and enough dressing to coat nicely. (You might not use all of the dressing.) Toss, taste, and adjust the seasoning with salt and pepper if necessary. Add a squeeze of lemon juice to brighten the flavors, then toss in the herbs.

To serve, divide the pasta among individual warmed dishes, and grind some black pepper over each serving at the table.

PAIRING

Farro, Chicken, and Avocado Salad with Lime Vinaigrette (page 62)

VARIATIONS

Various salmon preparations can be substituted for the smoked fish; cured salmon (gravlax) or flaked poached salmon would be equally delicious. Smoked trout or whitefish would also work well.

Fresh green peas or thawed frozen *petits pois* can be used in place of the snow peas.

FLAVOR BUILDING

A julienne of red and/or yellow peppers would fit right into this salad, as would cooled poached shrimp or diced lobster meat. You might also top each serving with salmon roe or Sevruga caviar.

To take this dish in a different direction, add some ginger juice and replace the lemon juice and zest with equal quantities of lime juice and zest.

FETTUCCINE WITH BEEF BRAISED IN RED WINE

One day, while standing in the meat department of my local supermarket, it hit me that pot roast, that classic of American home cooking, would be the perfect starting point for a pasta sauce. I purchased a chuck eye roast and began experimenting, braising it in a mixture of red wine, tomato, and stock, not unlike the Italian counterpart of pot roast called *stracotto*, which means "slow-cooked." The orange zest and garlic in the sauce were inspired by another Italian convention, *gremolata*, which usually garnishes osso buco. SERVES 4 TO 6

¼ cup olive oil

1 stalk celery, coarsely chopped

1 medium onion, peeled and coarsely chopped

1 large carrot, peeled and coarsely chopped

6 garlic cloves, crushed with the side of a knife and peeled

2 cups Chicken Stock (page 31)

2¼ pounds boneless chuck pot roast, 1½ to 1¾ inches thick, trimmed of excess fat

Coarse salt

Freshly ground black pepper

1 cup full-bodied red wine, such as Chianti or a Tuscan table wine

1½ cups canned tomato puree

5 strips orange zest, removed with a vegetable peeler

3 thyme sprigs

1 bay leaf

12 ounces fresh fettuccine

Preheat the oven to 325°F.

Warm 2 tablespoons of the olive oil in a heavy-bottomed ovenproof saucepan set over medium heat. Add the celery, onions, carrots, and garlic, and sauté, stirring, until the vegetables are nicely caramelized, 8 to 10 minutes. Pour ½ cup of the stock into the pot. Raise the heat to high and bring the stock to a boil, stirring to loosen any flavorful bits on the bottom of the pan. Transfer the contents of the pan to a bowl and set aside.

Wipe out the pan and return it to the stove. Pour the remaining 2 tablespoons oil into the pan and heat it over medium-high heat. Season the meat with salt and pepper, add it to the pan, and sear on all sides until well browned, 5 to 6 minutes per side. Transfer the meat to the bowl with the vegetables.

Deglaze the pan with the red wine, scraping up all the flavorful bits. Simmer until the wine is reduced by two-thirds, approximately 10 minutes.

Add the tomato puree, remaining 1½ cups chicken stock, orange zest, thyme, and bay leaf to the pan.

Return the meat and vegetables to the pan and season lightly with salt and pepper. Raise the heat to high and bring the liquid to a simmer. Cover the pan, transfer it to the oven, and braise until the meat is tender, about 2 hours. Check periodically to be sure that the liquid is just barely simmering. If it's bubbling aggressively, lower the temperature by 25 degrees.

After the meat has cooked for 1¾ hours, bring a large pot of salted water to a boil. (If you are making the sauce in advance, do this when you are ready to reheat the sauce and serve the pasta.)

Transfer the meat to a platter. Strain the sauce through a fine-mesh sieve set over a saucepan, pressing down on the solids to extract as much flavorful liquid as possible. Let the sauce stand for 5 minutes; then use a large spoon to skim off and discard any fat that has risen to the surface. Taste. If necessary, reduce the sauce slightly over high heat to thicken it and concentrate the flavors. Taste again, and adjust the seasoning if necessary.

When the meat is cool enough to handle, shred it, using the tines of a fork. Stir the meat into the sauce and warm it through gently over low heat.

The sauce can be made to this point, cooled, covered, and refrigerated for up to 2 days.

Add the fettuccine to the boiling water and cook until al dente, 2 to 3 minutes. Drain.

To serve, spoon some fettuccine onto each warmed plate, and spoon some sauce over each serving, taking care to include a good mix of beef and vegetables in each spoonful.

VARIATIONS

Rigatoni or pappardelle would be fine alternatives to the fettuccine.

Veal shanks (braised for 2 to 2½ hours) or pork shoulder (braised for approximately 2½ hours) would be equally good stand-ins for the beef.

PENNE WITH SWEET SAUSAGE, FONTINA, SAGE, AND DANDELION GREENS

The aromas of Fontina cheese and sage will make this sauce's presence known throughout the house the moment you toss the ingredients together in the kitchen. I'm especially fond of this dish because it uses one of my favorite child-hood ingredients, dandelion greens. When I was a kid, my sister and I dug up this bitter, slightly peppery green from the roadsides for my mother to clean and use in her cooking. They still grow wild today (a euphemistic way of saying that they are a weed), but cultivated ones are widely available. Seek out those that are less than 8 inches long; they're the least bitter of the batch. (Do not use garden dandelions, which may well have been sprayed with herbicide or fertilizer). SERVES 4 TO 6

Coarse salt

2 tablespoons olive oil

10 ounces sweet Italian sausage (2 to 3 small links), removed from its casing(s)

1 pound dried penne

¾ cup diced onion

1 tablespoon finely chopped garlic

4 sage leaves, cut into a chiffonade

1 cup dry white wine

½ cup Chicken Stock (page 31)

½ cup heavy cream

2 bunches dandelion greens, thick stems removed and discarded, leaves washed, dried, and chopped

8 ounces Fontina cheese, 6 ounces grated, the remainder left intact for grating at the table

Freshly ground black pepper

Set a large pot of salted water over high heat and bring it to a boil while you begin making the sauce.

Heat 1 tablespoon of the olive oil in a wide, deep-sided sauté pan set over medium heat. Add the sausage and sauté, stirring and breaking up the meat with a wooden spoon, just until the meat loses its pink color, 3 to 4 minutes. Use a slotted spoon to transfer the meat to a plate. Set aside.

By now, the water should be boiling. Add the pasta and cook until al dente, about 8 minutes, while you finish making the sauce.

Add the remaining 1 tablespoon oil to the pan and let it heat for a few seconds. Add the onions and cook, stirring, until softened but not browned, about 4 minutes. Add the garlic and sage and cook for 2 minutes more. Return the sausage to the pan, add the wine, and stir. Raise the heat to high, bring the wine to a boil, and continue to boil until reduced by about half, approximately 4 minutes. Add the stock and cream, and cook for 2 minutes.

By now, the pasta should be done. Drain it in a colander and immediately add it to the pan containing the sauce. Add the dandelion greens and toss well. As soon as the greens have just begun to wilt, stir in the grated Fontina, stirring it to help it melt and become pleasingly stringy. Season to taste with salt and lots of pepper.

To serve, transfer the pasta to a large warmed serving bowl and present it family-style from the center of the table. Pass the remaining Fontina alongside, with a grater, inviting everyone to grate extra cheese over his or her serving.

VARIATIONS

The Fontina cheese and dandelions would stand up admirably to hot Italian sausage. Or, as with most pastas using sausage, you might elect to make your own.

Mezze (half) rigatoni, with its tubular shape and ridges, would be a good replacement for the penne.

Rosemary or thyme can be used in place of the sage.

FLAVOR BUILDING

Pan-roasted radicchio (page 137) would fit right into this dish, adding bitterness and a gentle crunch.

RIGATONI WITH A SIRLOIN AND SAUSAGE SAUCE

Most Italian ragùs, or meat sauces, require hours of patient simmering, during which tomatoes break down, liquefy, and thicken, the flavor of the slow-cooked beef infuses the sauce, and the unmistakable scent of garlic wafts through the air, filling the house with aroma and anticipation. This unusually quick ragù owes its depth of flavor not to long cooking, but to carefully selected ingredients that make a fast impression (hot sausage and ground sirloin) and thicken the sauce instantly (butter, cream, cheese), offering all the charms of a homemade, slow-cooked sauce without advance planning or patient monitoring. SERVES 6 AS AN APPETIZER OR 4 AS A MAIN COURSE

Coarse salt

8 ounces (2 small links) hot Italian sausage, removed from its casing(s)

12 ounces ground sirloin

Freshly ground black pepper

½ cup diced onion

1 teaspoon minced garlic

12 ounces dried rigatoni

1 cup red wine

1 cup canned tomato puree

¾ cup Chicken Stock (page 31)

¼ cup heavy cream

2 tablespoons unsalted butter

½ cup finely grated Parmigiano-Reggiano, plus more for serving

¼ cup chopped flat-leaf parsley

Fill a large, heavy-bottomed pot with salted water. Set it over high heat and bring it to a boil while you begin making the sauce.

Put the sausage and sirloin in a bowl, season with salt and pepper, and gently mix. Set a wide, deep-sided, heavy-bottomed sauté pan over medium-high heat and let it warm up for 2 to 3 minutes. Then add the meat to the pan and cook, stirring, until lightly browned, about 5 minutes. Use a slotted spoon to transfer the meat to a bowl and set it aside.

Add the onions to the pan and cook, stirring, until softened and lightly browned, approximately 4 minutes. Add the garlic and cook for another minute.

By this time, the salted water should be boiling. Add the rigatoni and cook until al dente, 10 to 12 minutes, while you finish the sauce.

Add the wine to the pan and raise the heat to high. Cook, stirring to loosen any flavorful bits stuck to the bottom of the pan, until the wine comes to a boil and is reduced

by two-thirds, 5 to 6 minutes. Stir in the tomato puree and the stock, and return the meat to the pan. Bring the liquids to a boil, then lower the heat and let the sauce simmer for 5 minutes. Stir in the cream and cook for 2 more minutes. Taste the sauce, and adjust the seasoning with salt and pepper if necessary. Stir in the butter.

Drain the pasta and add it to the pan. Add the cheese and parsley, and toss.

To serve, divide the pasta among individual warmed plates or bowls, and pass additional grated Parmigiano alongside.

RIGATONI WITH CRACKED BLACK PEPPER, BASIL, AND FRESH RICOTTA

In this loose adaptation of a classic Italian dish, a touch of cream added to ricotta cheese effortlessly turns it into a rich and homogenous sauce. Against this backdrop, a trio of complementary ingredients—black pepper, basil, and, Parmigiano-Reggiano, all of which are usually called on as finishing touches—become the center of attention. As with any recipe that features only a handful of ingredients, the quality of each one is crucial here.

Note that you want *cracked* rather than ground black pepper here; adjust the tension on your mill's knob if possible, or use a mortar and pestle to crack whole peppercorns. SERVES 4

Coarse salt

12 ounces dried rigatoni

¼ cup heavy cream

2/3 cup fresh ricotta cheese

4 teaspoons chopped chives

¼ cup basil chiffonade

8 ounces Parmigiano-Reggiano, 1 cup grated, the rest left intact for grating at the table

2 teaspoons cracked black pepper

¼ cup extra virgin olive oil

4 teaspoons minced garlic

Set a large pot of salted water over high heat and bring it to a boil. Add the rigatoni and cook until al dente, about 10 minutes.

Meanwhile, pour the cream into a small pot and warm it over low heat. Put the ricotta in a bowl, and whisk in the warmed cream. Add half the chives, half the basil, and the grated Parmigiano. Season with salt and the cracked pepper.

Heat 2 tablespoons of the olive oil in a sauté pan set over medium-high heat. Add the garlic and sauté until it turns golden, approximately 2 minutes. Drain the rigatoni, add it to the pan, add the remaining 2 tablespoons oil, and toss. Season to taste with salt.

Toss the pasta with half of the ricotta/herb mixture, and divide it among individual warmed plates or bowls. Spoon some of the remaining mixture over each serving, sprinkle with the rest of the basil and chives, and serve. Pass the remaining Parmigiano at the table, with a grater, inviting everyone to grate extra cheese over his or her serving.

SPAGHETTI WITH HOT AND SWEET PEPPERS

Originally intended as a late-summer recipe that uses a variety of peppers from the garden, this pasta dish would also be perfectly appropriate and pleasing at other times of year. Use as many different peppers as you can get your hands on; the greater the variety, the more interesting it will be to the palate and the eye. This is a very beautiful sauce, even as it's being cooked; the multicolored peppers in the pan are captivating, an indication of how they will taste in the finished dish. SERVES 4

¼ cup plus 2 tablespoons extra virgin olive oil

1 medium onion, peeled and thinly sliced

1½ pounds mixed hot and sweet peppers (ideally 2 red bell, 1 yellow bell, 1 orange bell, 2 hot Italian, and 2 jalapeño), seeded and julienned

1 tablespoon minced garlic

Coarse salt

Freshly ground black pepper

¾ cup Chicken Stock (page 31)

1 pound dried spaghetti

2 tablespoons basil chiffonade

Parmigiano-Reggiano, for serving

Heat the ¼ cup olive oil in a wide, deep sauté pan set over medium-high heat. Add the onions and sauté until softened but not browned, approximately 5 minutes. Add the peppers and garlic, and season with salt and pepper. Cook over medium-low heat, stirring often, until the vegetables just begin to soften, 10 to 12 minutes. Add the stock, bring it to a boil over high heat, and let it continue to boil and reduce for 5 minutes.

Meanwhile, bring a pot of salted water to a boil. Add the spaghetti and cook until al dente, about 8 minutes. Drain.

Season the sauce with salt and pepper. Add the spaghetti, drizzle with the remaining 2 tablespoons oil, and toss.

Transfer the pasta and sauce to a warmed serving bowl, garnish with the basil, and serve family-style, passing the cheese alongside.

PAIRING

Grilled Marinated Pork Chops (page 176)

VARIATION

This proportion of hot peppers makes a spicy sauce, so adjust it to accommodate your own taste.

FLAVOR BUILDING

A number of traditional Italian ingredients fit right in here, such as crushed toasted bread crumbs (page 111), dried oregano, and/or 1 pound of sausage meat. Summer savory would also be a good addition.

RISOTTO WITH PANCETTA, BIBB LETTUCE, PEAS, AND MINT

While working in French restaurants, I learned to braise soft lettuces and to sauté them in a scant quantity of butter in order to serve them as a vegetable. I found the effect beguiling. The greens—which I had previously thought of only as components of a salad or sandwich—took on a whole new character, becoming elegant and alluring. Since then, I've found endless applications for wilting lettuces and other greens, such as arugula and pea shoots, into pastas and risottos. I had never used Bibb lettuce in this way until I was developing recipes for this book, and I found it to be the perfect fit. SERVES 6 AS AN APPETIZER OR 4 AS A MAIN COURSE

2 quarts Chicken Stock (page 31)

Coarse salt

1 cup green peas or frozen *petits pois*, thawed

6 ounces pancetta, cut into ¼-inch dice

1 tablespoon olive oil

1 medium onion, peeled and cut into small dice

4 garlic cloves, peeled and minced

1 pound (2 cups) Canaroli or Vialone Nano rice

¼ cup dry white wine

½ cup grated Parmigiano-Reggiano, plus more for passing at the table

2 heads Bibb lettuce, cut lengthwise into wide strips

4 tablespoons (½ stick) cold unsalted butter, cut into small cubes

About 4 teaspoons freshly squeezed lemon juice

2 tablespoons chopped flat-leaf parsley

2 teaspoons chopped mint leaves

Freshly ground black pepper to taste

Pour the chicken stock into a saucepan and bring it to a simmer over medium heat. Keep the stock at a low simmer.

While the stock is heating, bring a saucepan of slightly salted water to a boil. Fill a large bowl halfway with ice water. Add the peas to the boiling water and cook them for 1 minute. Use a slotted spoon to transfer them to the ice water to stop the cooking and preserve their color. Drain them and set them aside.

Put the pancetta and the olive oil in a large, heavy-bottomed pot, and set it over medium heat. Sauté, stirring, until the pancetta is lightly crisp and has rendered enough fat to generously coat the bottom of the pot, about 6 minutes. Remove the pancetta with a slotted spoon and set it on a paper towel–lined plate.

Add the onions to the pot and sauté until softened but not browned, approximately 4 minutes. Then add the garlic and sauté for 1 minute. Add the rice and cook, stirring, for 7 to 8 minutes. Add the wine and cook, stirring, until it is almost completely absorbed, 2 minutes.

Add about 1 cup of the simmering stock to the rice. Cook for approximately 2 minutes, stirring often, until the stock is almost completely absorbed. Gradually add more stock, a cup at a time, stirring gently until it is absorbed by the rice before adding the next cup.

After about 15 minutes, begin tasting the rice and adding the stock judiciously, in smaller increments. The rice should be firm yet cooked through in 18 to 20 minutes. When the risotto is done, it will be creamy but still firm to the bite.

Return the pancetta to the pot and stir it into the risotto. Stir in the grated cheese, peas, and lettuce. Then stir in the butter, 1 piece at a time. Cook, stirring, for 2 minutes.

Remove the pot from the heat and stir in the lemon juice, a little at a time, just until the risotto takes on a bright lemon flavor. Then stir in the parsley and mint. Season to taste with salt and pepper.

To serve, divide the risotto among individual warmed plates or large, shallow bowls, and pass extra grated Parmigiano alongside.

VARIATIONS

Other soft lettuces, like butter, oak leaf, and Lolla Rossa, can be substituted for the Bibb.

Using diced slab bacon in place of the pancetta will yield a nice smoky result.

SHRIMP RISOTTO WITH SWEET PEAS, LEEKS, AND CHERVIL

This risotto sports a surprisingly light touch, thanks to the distinctly springtime combination of tender pink shrimp, pale green and yellow leeks, delicate peas, and a pronounced lemony undercurrent. The gentle flavor of chervil, one of my favorite herbs, fits right into this context. SERVES 4

2 quarts Chicken Stock (page 31)

Coarse salt to taste

1 cup freshly shelled green peas or frozen *petits pois,* thawed

4 small leeks, white and light green parts only, thickly sliced on the diagonal, rinsed, and drained

3 tablespoons olive oil

½ cup diced onion

2 teaspoons finely chopped garlic

1 teaspoon ground coriander

1 pound (2 cups) Canaroli or Vialone Nano rice

½ cup dry white wine

12 to 14 large shrimp, peeled and deveined

Freshly ground black pepper to taste

2 tablespoons unsalted butter

¼ cup heavy cream

About 4 teaspoons freshly squeezed lemon juice

¼ cup chopped flat-leaf parsley

¼ cup chopped chervil leaves

Pour the chicken stock into a saucepan and bring it to a simmer over medium heat. Keep the stock at a low simmer.

While the stock is heating, bring a pot of lightly salted water to a boil. Fill a large bowl halfway with ice water. Add the peas to the boiling water and blanch them for 1 to 2 minutes. Use a slotted spoon to transfer them to the ice water to stop the cooking and set their color.

Add the leeks to the boiling water and cook until tender, 2 minutes. Use a slotted spoon to transfer the leeks to the ice water. Drain the vegetables and set them aside.

Warm 2 tablespoons of the olive oil in large, heavy-bottomed pot set over medium-low heat. Add the onions and sauté for 2 minutes. Then add the garlic and coriander, and cook for another minute. Add the rice and sauté until coated with fat and glossy. Add the wine and cook, stirring, until it is almost completely absorbed, 3 minutes.

Add about 1 cup of the simmering stock to the rice. Cook for approximately 2 minutes, stirring often, until the stock is almost completely absorbed. Gradually add more stock, a cup at a time, stirring gently until it is absorbed by the rice before adding the next cup. After about 15 minutes, begin tasting the rice and adding the stock judiciously, in smaller increments. The rice should be firm yet cooked through in 18 to 20 minutes. When the risotto is done, it will be creamy but still firm to the bite.

Meanwhile, heat the remaining 1 tablespoon oil in a sauté pan set over medium heat. Season the shrimp with salt and pepper, add them to the pan, and sauté until firm and pink, about 3 minutes.

Add the peas, leeks, and shrimp to the risotto. Stir in the butter and cream. Stir in the lemon juice, a little at a time, until the risotto takes on a nice bright flavor, then stir in the parsley, and 2 tablespoons of the chervil. Season to taste.

To serve, divide the risotto among individual warmed shallow bowls or dinner plates. If using, finish each serving with a scattering of the remaining chervil.

PAIRING

Shaved Fennel, Green Apple, and Pecorino Romano Salad (page 28)

VARIATIONS

Chopped cooked lobster meat can be used in place of the shrimp.

This risotto would also be delicious with no shellfish at all, perhaps as a side dish to fish or chicken.

Basil has a great affinity with lemon; replace the parsley and chervil with chopped basil.

ROASTED TOMATO RISOTTO

Here ripe tomatoes are roasted with garlic and thyme to concentrate their flavor, then stirred into a risotto where they all but melt right in. Finished with a touch of cream and Parmesan cheese, this is a deceptively simple looking dish that's rich with flavor. Bacon contributes an important counterpoint, grounding the dish with its smoky flavor. SERVES 6 AS AN APPETIZER OR 4 AS A MAIN COURSE

1½ pounds ripe beefsteak tomatoes or mixed heirloom tomatoes, halved and seeded

2 tablespoons extra virgin olive oil

1 teaspoon thyme leaves

2 garlic cloves, peeled and thinly sliced, plus 1 teaspoon minced garlic

Coarse salt

Freshly ground black pepper

1½ quarts Chicken Stock (page 31)

2 ounces slab bacon, cut into ¼-inch dice

½ cup minced onion

1 pound (2 cups) Canaroli or Vialone Nano rice

½ cup dry white wine

3 tablespoons heavy cream

1 cup grated Parmigiano-Reggiano, plus more for serving

½ cup basil chiffonade

3 tablespoons minced chives

Preheat the oven to 400°F.

Put the tomatoes, cut side down, in a small roasting pan or on a cookie sheet. Drizzle them with 1 tablespoon of the olive oil; then scatter the thyme and sliced garlic over them. Season with salt and pepper.

Roast the tomatoes in the oven until softened and fragrant, approximately 12 minutes. Remove them from the oven and set them aside to cool a bit. When they are cool enough to handle, remove the skins (they should slip off easily) and transfer the tomatoes to a bowl, along with any juice that has accumulated in the pan. Set aside.

While the tomatoes are cooling, pour the chicken stock into a saucepan and bring it to a simmer. Keep the stock at a low simmer.

In a large, heavy-bottomed saucepan, heat the remaining, 1 tablespoon oil over medium heat. Add the bacon and sauté until lightly browned, approximately 4 minutes. Add the onions and cook, stirring, until softened but not browned, approximately 6 minutes. Add the minced garlic and cook until fragrant, approximately 2 more minutes. Add the rice and sauté until it is coated with fat and glossy. Add the wine and cook, stirring, until it is almost completely absorbed, 3 minutes.

Add about 1 cup of the simmering stock to the rice. Cook for about 2 minutes, stirring often, until the stock is almost completely absorbed. Gradually add more stock, a cup at a time, stirring gently until it is absorbed by the rice before adding the next cup. After about 15 minutes, begin tasting the rice and adding the stock judiciously, in smaller increments. The rice should be firm yet cooked through in 18 to 20 minutes total. When the risotto is done, it will be creamy but still firm to the bite.

Stir the tomatoes into the risotto. Then stir in the cream and 1 cup Parmigiano. Taste, and season with salt and pepper. Stir for another minute; then stir in the basil and chives. Spoon the risotto into deep warmed pasta bowls, and serve with extra cheese on the side.

PAIRING

Salmon with Red Wine and Balsamic Vinegar (page 158)

FLAVOR BUILDING

Sliced pitted black olives are a good addition. For a special-occasion dish, omit the cheese and olives and stir cooked shrimp into this risotto.

RISOTTO WITH SAUSAGE, RADICCHIO, AND PECORINO ROMANO

This rustic, almost primal Italian dish is made with hot Italian sausage, producing a wonderfully spicy, garlicky risotto. The heat is transmitted through the entire dish because the rendered sausage fat, rather than butter or oil, is the cooking medium for the onions, garlic, and rice. If you prefer a milder risotto, use sweet sausage or a combination of sweet and hot. The technique given here for cooking radicchio approximates the flavor produced by grilling but allows the leaves to maintain more of their natural color and texture. SERVES 6 AS AN APPETIZER OR 4 AS A MAIN COURSE

¼ cup olive oil, plus more if needed

1 medium head radicchio, cut into ½-inch-thick wedges

Coarse salt

Freshly ground black pepper

2 quarts Chicken Stock (page 31)

4 links hot Italian sausages (1 pound total), removed from their casings

½ cup diced onion (small dice)

3 garlic cloves, minced

1 pound (2 cups) Canaroli or Vialone Nano rice

½ cup dry white wine

¼ cup chopped, flat-leaf parsley

¼ cup grated pecorino Romano, plus more for serving

1 tablespoon unsalted butter

Heat 2 tablespoons of the olive oil in a sauté pan set over medium-high heat. Add the radicchio, season with salt and pepper, and sauté until lightly browned on both sides. Transfer the radicchio to a bowl, cover with plastic, and let it steam in its own heat for 15 minutes.

While the radicchio is steaming, pour the chicken stock into a saucepan and bring it to a simmer. Keep the stock at a low simmer.

Remove the radicchio from the bowl, and when it is cool, trim away the core and cut it into large dice. Set aside.

Heat the remaining 2 tablespoons oil in a heavy-bottomed 2-quart saucepan set over medium-high heat. Add the sausage and lightly brown it, breaking it up with a wooden spoon, approximately 6 minutes. Use a slotted spoon to transfer the sausage to a bowl and set it aside.

Add the onions to the saucepan and sauté, adding 1 tablespoon olive oil if necessary, for 4 minutes. Add the garlic and cook for 1 more minute. Add the rice and sauté until it is coated with fat and glossy, 7 to 8

minutes. Add the wine and stir until it is completely absorbed by the rice, 3 minutes.

Add about 1 cup of the simmering stock to the rice. Cook for about 2 minutes, stirring often, until the stock is almost completely absorbed. Gradually add more stock, a cup at a time, stirring gently until it is absorbed by the rice before adding the next cup. After about 15 minutes, begin tasting the rice and adding the stock judiciously, in smaller increments. The rice should be firm yet cooked through in 18 to 20 minutes. When the risotto is done, it will be creamy but still firm to the bite.

Stir the sausage, radicchio, parsley, and pecorino into the risotto. Stir in the butter. Taste, and adjust the seasoning with salt and pepper if necessary. Divide the risotto among individual warmed plates or bowls, grate some more cheese over the top, and serve at once.

MAIN COURSES

THE RECIPES FOR THESE MAIN COURSE DISHES offer a more complex flavor than their ease of preparation might suggest. In developing them, I revisited some techniques from cooking school—a logical source of inspiration because culinary students learn fundamental recipes and techniques that can be turned into something new and unexpected with a few simple changes or additions. Among the ideas drawn from this well are the use of compound butters, as in the Roast Cod with Escargot Butter, and the classic method of cooking fish in parchment, as in Asian Striped Bass *en Papillote*.

Many of these recipes also employ techniques that add or intensify flavor with no extra work. For example, marinades and dry rubs help flavors penetrate fish, poultry, or meat, and grilling intensifies the flavor of the central ingredient. Another efficient technique is slow cooking, which produces both the central component and an accompaniment in one pot, as in Braised Pork with Fennel and Red Bliss Potatoes.

Then there are those recipes based on dishes that qualify as home cooking in their country of origin, such as Chicken with Olives and Preserved Lemon Sauce and Duck Vindaloo. There's even a nod to the United States in the Roast Cod with a New England Chowder Sauce.

STEAMED CLAMS WITH CHORIZO, CHILES, AND CILANTRO

One night, Helen surprised me by announcing that the two of us were going to have dinner on the beach. This sounded great, but my expectations were confused when she made for the truck carrying nothing but a stockpot, a bottle of chilled white Burgundy, and an armful of firewood.

At the beach, Helen built a small fire in the sand. We set up two folding chairs and sipped wine as the sun set and the fire burned down. As dinnertime approached, she dug a shallow hole, placed a grate over the impromptu pit, set the pot over the flame, and grilled some bread on the little free space left on this makeshift grill. When she lifted the lid from the pot, the aroma was intoxicating. She then revealed that she had precooked a stew of onions, garlic, sausage, and wine, let it cool, and then added clams to the pot. All that was left to do at the beach was to reheat the base, let the clams steam open, then ladle the shellfish and broth over slices of grilled bread in each bowl.

You can replicate the make-ahead nature of this recipe at home—or make it *à la minute,* which doesn't take very long at all. SERVES 4

6 ounces chorizo sausage, casing removed

3 tablespoons extra virgin olive oil

1 cup diced onion

1 tablespoon plus 1 teaspoon minced garlic

1 hot red chile pepper, such as Anaheim, red Italian, Fresno, or cherry, cut crosswise in thin slices

1 cup dry white wine

Coarse salt

Freshly ground black pepper

1 baguette, cut on the diagonal into eight ½-inch-thick slices

4 pounds littleneck or Manila clams, scrubbed and rinsed

2 tablespoons chopped cilantro leaves

In a pot for which you have a lid, heat the chorizo and 1 tablespoon of the olive oil over medium-low heat until the chorizo renders enough fat to generously coat the bottom of the pot, about 4 minutes. Add the onions and sauté until softened but not browned, about 4 minutes. Add the garlic and chiles, and sauté for 1 minute. Add the wine, raise the heat to high, bring it to a boil, and let it boil until reduced by two-thirds, about 5 minutes. Season lightly with salt and pepper to taste.

The recipe can be made to this point, then cooled, covered, and refrigerated, on the morning of the day you plan to serve it. Reheat gently before proceeding.

Add the clams to the pot over medium heat and cover it. Let the clams steam until they open, about 3 minutes. Scatter the cilantro over the clams just before serving.

Drizzle the remaining 2 tablespoons olive oil over the bread slices. Season with salt and pepper, and grill or toast on each side.

To serve, put 2 croutons in the bottom of each of four warmed bowls and ladle some clams and broth over them.

ASIAN STRIPED BASS *EN PAPILLOTE*

This recipe employs a classic French technique that cooks fish with vegetables, herbs, and/or wine in a parchment-paper parcel. Much prized for its beauty—the packets are often presented and cut open right at the table—*en papillote* is, above all, an efficient way to cook the fish and create the sauce in one fell swoop. The fish is steamed as much as it is baked, resulting in a pure, clean taste that makes it a logical platform for Asian flavors, achieved here with the addition of ginger, cilantro, and soy sauce. SERVES 4

8 scallions, white part thinly sliced crosswise, green tops reserved

12 cilantro sprigs, leaves removed and chopped, stems reserved

4 striped bass fillets
(7 ounces each)

Coarse salt

Freshly ground white pepper

1 teaspoon grated lemon zest, plus 2 tablespoons freshly squeezed lemon juice

4 tablespoons (½ stick) unsalted butter

1 teaspoon ginger juice

3 tablespoons light sesame oil or walnut oil

¼ cup soy sauce

Preheat the oven to 450°F.

Prepare four 10-inch squares of parchment paper or aluminum foil, and fold each in half. In the center of each piece, make a bed of scallion tops and cilantro stems. Season the fish fillets on both sides with salt and pepper, and place 1 fillet on top of each herb bed. Scatter the lemon zest over the fish, and top each fillet with 1 tablespoon of the butter.

In a small bowl, whisk together the lemon juice, ginger juice, sesame oil, and soy sauce. Spoon the mixture over the fish. Fold the squares in half diagonally and seal all the edges by crimping them together. Put the packets on a cookie sheet.

Put the sheet in the oven and bake until the packets puff slightly, 8 minutes for thinner fillets, 10 minutes for thicker. Remove the packets from the oven.

To serve, cut open each *papillote,* being careful not to spill any liquids and avoiding the hot steam that may escape as you open it. Use a slotted spatula to transfer 1 fillet to each of four warmed dinner plates, leaving the herbs behind. Pour the cooking liquid from the packets into a bowl, and spoon some over and around the fish on each plate. Scatter the chopped cilantro and sliced scallions over the fish, and serve immediately.

PAIRING

Sautéed Spinach with Garlic, Ginger, and Sesame Oil (page 199)

VARIATION

The striped bass can be replaced with flounder, cod, or halibut.

FLAVOR BUILDING

Add some thinly sliced fresh chiles to the beds of scallion and cilantro, or drizzle them with chili oil instead of sesame oil for a spicier dish. Or season the fish with Chinese five-spice powder and add thinly sliced garlic and/or lemongrass to the beds of vegetables.

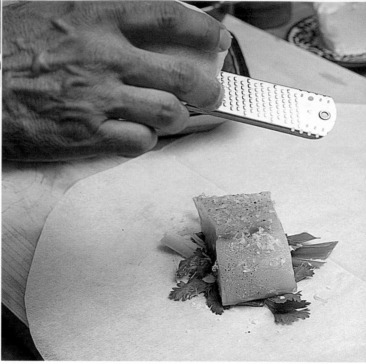

Make a bed of scallions and cilantro on a 10-inch circle of parchment paper. Place the striped bass on top.

Scatter the lemon zest over the fish.

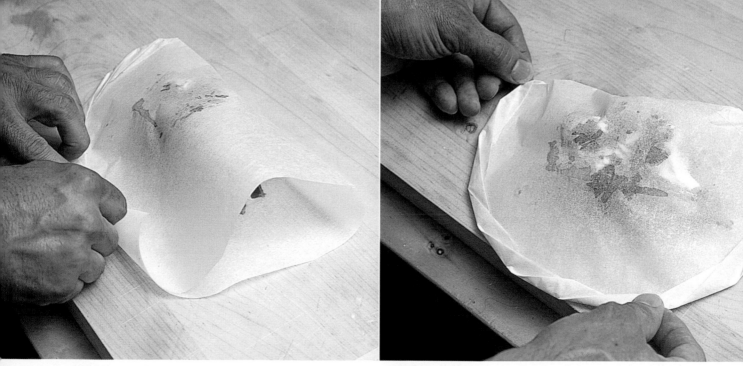

Fold the parchment paper in half.

Crimp the edges to seal. Put the packets on a shallow pan and bake until the packets puff slightly, 8 to 10 minutes.

Spoon the lemon juice, ginger juice, soy sauce, and oil mixture over the fish.

Top each fillet with 1 tablespoon of butter.

Cut open each *papillote* with scissors; be careful not to spill any liquid.

Transfer the fish to a warm dinner plate. Spoon the sauce over each serving.

ROASTED WILD STRIPED BASS WITH LEEKS, FINGERLING POTATOES, AND LEMON

In writing this book, I turned to a number of reliable methods for efficiently cooking fish, including baking it in a sealed vessel, making a pan sauce from what remains in the pan after it's been cooked, and steaming it atop a bed of vegetables. This recipe uses all three techniques. The ingredients list is short, but each one is maximized through the various techniques used here. SERVES 4

Coarse salt

2 leeks, white part only, cut on the diagonal into ¼-inch-thick slices (1 cup sliced)

8 fingerling or Red Bliss potatoes

4 wild striped bass fillets (6 ounces each)

Freshly ground black pepper

¼ cup plus 2 tablespoons extra virgin olive oil

2 cups bottled clam juice

2 strips lemon zest removed with a vegetable peeler, cut lengthwise into thin strips, plus 1 tablespoon freshly squeezed lemon juice, plus more if needed

4 thyme sprigs

2 tablespoons chopped chervil or parsley

Preheat the oven to 400°F.

Bring a pot of salted water to a boil. Fill a medium bowl halfway with ice water.

Add the leeks to the boiling water and blanch them for 1 minute. Use a slotted spoon to transfer them to the ice water to stop the cooking and preserve their beautiful color. Strain, and set aside in a bowl.

Add the potatoes to the boiling water, and boil until tender (a sharp, thin-bladed knife, will easily pierce to the center, approximately 12 minutes). Remove the potatoes with a slotted spoon, and set them aside to cool. When they are cool enough to handle, slice the potatoes into ¼-inch-thick rounds and add them to the bowl containing the leeks.

Divide the leeks and potatoes into four "beds" in a roasting pan, arranging them without crowding. Season the fillets on both sides with salt and pepper, and place them on top of the vegetables. Drizzle with the 2 tablespoons olive oil. Heat the pan over high heat for 2 minutes.

Add the clam juice, lemon zest, lemon juice, and thyme to the pan, and bring the liquid to a boil over high heat. Remove the pan from the heat, cover it tightly with aluminum foil, and transfer it to the oven. Bake until the fish is just opaque in the center, about 8 minutes.

Remove the pan from the oven. Using one or two spatulas, carefully remove the fish, with their beds of leeks and potatoes, and place a stack on each of four warmed dinner plates. Cover each serving loosely with foil to keep it warm.

Discard the thyme sprigs. Pour the liquid from the roasting pan into a saucepan and bring it to a boil over high heat. Continue to boil until the liquid is lightly thickened and flavorful, about 2 minutes. Whisk in the remaining ¼ cup oil, and remove the pot from the heat. Taste the sauce, and adjust the seasoning with salt, pepper, and more lemon juice if necessary. Stir in the chervil.

To serve, spoon some sauce over and around the fish and vegetables on each plate.

VARIATIONS

Black sea bass, grouper, and Atlantic salmon would all be good substitutes for the wild striped bass in this dish.

FLAVOR BUILDING

Add a thinly sliced fennel bulb to the pot with the leeks, and finish the dish with a scattering of chopped fennel fronds.

Sprinkle some cracked coriander over the fish along with the salt and pepper.

Replace the chervil with a few rosemary branches.

ROAST COD WITH A
NEW ENGLAND CHOWDER SAUCE

New Yorkers are loyal to hometown sports teams, pizza, and cheesecake. But when it comes to chowder, many of us are turncoats: rather than championing the brothy, tomato-based Manhattan clam chowder, we opt for the cream-based New England variety. Thick with potato and with a pronounced smoky salinity from the salt pork that classically starts the dish, the *other* chowder has more going for it on every level—New York's is basically just a vegetable soup with clams.

This main course grew out of my fondness for New England clam chowder, turning it into a sauce for one of that region's most beloved catches, cod. The conversion is pretty straightforward, using less cream than you would for soup, thinning and flavoring it with the juices released when the shellfish is steamed open. You can make this with small, tender Manila clams or relatively plump littlenecks. SERVES 4

24 Manila or 16 littleneck clams, scrubbed

2 ounces slab bacon, diced

1 teaspoon canola oil

½ cup diced onion (small dice)

½ cup diced leek (small dice)

1 teaspoon finely chopped garlic

4 medium Red Bliss potatoes, peeled and diced (about 1 cup diced)

1 cup heavy cream

Coarse salt

Freshly ground white pepper to taste

4 skin-on cod fillets (6 ounces each)

2 tablespoons olive oil

1 tablespoon finely chopped flat-leaf parsley

Place the clams and 1 tablespoon water in a saucepan, cover, and steam over high heat until the clams open, 4 to 5 minutes. Set aside 8 clams in their shells for garnish. Remove the remaining clams from their shells. (Discard any clams that do not open.) Strain the liquid from the pot through a fine-mesh sieve set over a bowl, and set the broth aside.

Put the bacon and canola oil in a large, heavy-bottomed pot and sauté over medium-low heat until the bacon is browned and crisp and has rendered some fat, about 6 minutes. Use tongs or a slotted spoon to transfer the bacon to a paper towel–lined plate.

Add the onions to the pot and sauté until they are softened but not browned, about 4 minutes. Add the leeks and garlic, and sauté until softened but not browned, about 2 minutes. Return the bacon to the pot and add the potatoes, cream, and reserved clam juice. Lightly season the contents of the pot with

salt and pepper. Raise the heat to high, bring the broth to a boil, then lower the heat and let it simmer for 10 minutes.

Remove the pot from the heat. Return the shelled and unshelled clams to the pot, and season to taste. Cover the pot to keep the sauce warm.

Heat the olive oil in a wide, deep sauté pan set over medium heat. Season the cod fillets with salt and pepper, and put them in the pan, skin side down, without crowding. Cook until golden, about 4 minutes, then turn and cook about 3 minutes more, depending on the thickness of the fish.

To serve, transfer the fillets to a warmed serving platter, and spoon the sauce over and around the fish. Arrange the unshelled clams around and on top of the fish, and scatter the parsley over the top.

PAIRINGS

Potato Puree (page 212), Escarole,
White Beans, and Apple-Smoked
Bacon (page 194)

VARIATIONS

Substitute other firm whitefish, such
as halibut or bass.

Use salt pork in place of the
bacon for a more traditional New
England chowder flavor.

FLAVOR BUILDING

Using double-smoked bacon will
infuse the entire sauce with a smoky
undercurrent; don't return the bacon
to the pot after it's been browned.
Instead, mince it and sprinkle some
of it over each serving.

ROAST COD WITH ESCARGOT BUTTER

When cooking in France, I learned to make a compound butter—a softened butter with herbs, wine, and/or seasoning stirred into it—with garlic, shallots, and parsley that was spooned over the snail in each compartment of an escargot dish just before baking. The butter melted into and around the escargot, imbuing it with rich flavor and filling each little indentation with a sauce that demanded to be soaked up with bread.

The butter featured in this recipe serves as a sauce for seared cod fillets. I've added some flavor builders here: diced prosciutto, Dijon mustard, and almond flour, which acts as a binding agent, causing the sauce to become emulsified. SERVES 4

ESCARGOT BUTTER

4 tablespoons (½ stick) unsalted butter, at room temperature

1½ tablespoons chopped flat-leaf parsley

1 large garlic clove, peeled and minced

2 teaspoons minced shallots

Freshly ground black pepper to taste

½ teaspoon Dijon mustard

1½ tablespoons minced prosciutto di Parma

1 tablespoon almond flour (see Note)

2 tablespoons freshly squeezed lemon juice

Heaping ¼ teaspoon coarse salt

2 tablespoons canola oil

4 cod fillets (7 ounces each), skin on

Coarse salt

Freshly ground black pepper

Preheat the oven to 450°F.

Combine all the ingredients for the escargot butter except the salt and pepper in a small bowl. Stir them together with a rubber spatula until thoroughly incorporated. Season with the pepper and set aside.

Heat the canola oil in a wide, deep, ovenproof sauté pan set over medium-high heat. Season the cod fillets with salt and pepper, add them to the pan, skinned side up, and cook for 4 minutes. Turn them over and cook on the other side for 1 minute. Slide the pan off the heat.

Spoon 1 tablespoon of the escargot butter over each fillet, put the pan in the oven, and bake until the fish is just cooked through and is opaque in the center, 2 to 3 minutes. Remove the pan from the oven.

To serve, use a spatula to transfer a cod fillet to each of four warmed dinner plates or shallow bowls. Swirl any remaining escargot butter and fish juices in the pan together, and pour them over the fish on each plate.

Note: Almond flour can be purchased at health food stores or made by grinding bleached almonds in a food processor.

PAIRINGS

Oven-Roasted Mushrooms (page 210), Potato Puree (page 212), Pan-Roasted Zucchini with Cilantro-Mint Gremolata (page 200)

VARIATIONS

The escargot butter will complement any firm white-fleshed fish, such as halibut, grouper, or sole.

The parsley in the butter can be replaced with other herbs, such as chives, chervil, tarragon, or basil.

FLAVOR BUILDING

Adding lemon zest, or a combination of lemon, lime, and orange zest, to the butter will punch up its flavor.

To echo the almond flour in the butter, add ¼ cup toasted slivered almonds or hazelnuts to it.

LIME AND BUTTER-BRAISED FLUKE

I've always appreciated fluke for its understated flavor and delicate texture, although it's sometimes so fragile that it can nearly disintegrate when cooked. Coiling fluke fillets improves their stamina in the oven and extends their cooking time. I first saw this moist cooking technique (it's nearly a braise) used with Dover sole when I was a saucier for the great French chef Jacques Maximin. SERVES 4

1½ pounds fluke fillet

4 tablespoons (½ stick) unsalted butter

¼ cup minced shallots

1 teaspoon minced garlic

Coarse salt

Freshly ground white pepper

1 cup dry white wine

2 tablespoons freshly squeezed lime juice, plus more if needed

1 bunch scallions (about 8 scallions), white part only, thinly sliced on the diagonal, optional

2 tablespoons chopped cilantro leaves, optional

Preheat the oven to 400°F.

Using a sharp knife, halve each fluke fillet lengthwise by cutting down the center but not all the way through, so it stays attached at the tail. Flatten the fillet into one piece with the flat surface facing downward, and roll it up (see page 154).

Butter an ovenproof baking pan with 1 tablespoon of the butter. Scatter the shallots and garlic around the pan. Season the fish with salt and pepper, and arrange them in the pan with the seams touching (to keep them from unfurling). Pour the wine and lime juice around the fish. Cover the pan tightly with aluminum foil and place it in the oven. Bake until the fillets are opaque in the center, 12 to 14 minutes. (Check for doneness by peeking between the seams of a fish with the help of a sharp knife. Err on the side of undercooking the fish; the carryover heat will finish cooking it out of the oven.)

Use a slotted spatula to transfer the fish to a warmed serving platter, and keep them covered and warm.

Pour the braising liquid into a small saucepan set over high heat. Bring it to a boil and continue to boil until the liquid has reduced and the flavors have become concentrated, about 2 minutes. Lower the heat and swirl in the remaining 3 tablespoons butter. Add the scallions and cilantro, if using. Taste, and adjust the seasoning with salt, pepper, and some more lime juice, if needed.

To serve, spoon the sauce over the fish and serve from the center of the table.

PAIRINGS

Potato Puree (page 212), Sautéed Shell Beans with Pancetta (page 204)

VARIATION

In place of the fluke, try lemon sole or Dover sole.

FLAVOR BUILDING

Top each serving with a teaspoonful of Osetra caviar for an opulent flourish.

Halve each fluke fillet lengthwise but not all the way through.

The fish should remain as one piece at the tail.

Flatten the fillet into one piece with the flat surface facing down.

Carefully roll the fish up.

The fish will look like a tight spiral. Continue as directed.

ROASTED HALIBUT
WITH LEMON-CAPER BUTTER

Classic French recipes are often known for more complex cooking methods than for timesaving tricks. But there are a few versatile techniques that deliver big flavors with little work. One of my favorites is compound butter, or butter that is softened and enhanced with wine, shallots, or herbs and used to sauce meats, fish, and vegetables.

Compound butters can be made in advance, rolled into a log, wrapped in plastic, and kept in the refrigerator or freezer for last-minute deployment. They're a great vehicle for experimentation, allowing you to create original butters to suit your own taste or perhaps to accompany, if not complete, a specific dish.

Here, a compound butter of shallots, parsley, lemon, garlic, and capers infuses roasted halibut with aromatic flavor. The almond flour (page 151) adds texture and holds the butter and flavors in emulsion. SERVES 4

8 tablespoons (1 stick) unsalted butter, softened at room temperature

4½ teaspoons almond flour

1 tablespoon finely chopped shallot

1 tablespoon finely chopped flat-leaf parsley

½ teaspoon finely chopped garlic mashed to a paste with a pinch of salt

1 tablespoon capers packed in brine, rinsed, dried, and chopped

½ teaspoon finely grated lemon zest

1 tablespoon freshly squeezed lemon juice

Coarse salt and freshly ground white pepper to taste

1 tablespoon canola oil

4 halibut fillets, 6 ounces each

Preheat the oven to 400°F.

Put the butter in a bowl. Add the almond flour, shallot, parsley, garlic, capers, lemon zest, and lemon juice. Combine the ingredients with a rubber spatula and season with salt and pepper. You can prepare the butter in advance: Transfer to a sheet of plastic wrap, roll into a cylinder about 4 inches long and 1 inch in diameter, wrap tightly, and refrigerate for up to 1 day or freeze for up to 2 months. Allow the butter to thaw and soften before proceeding.

Heat the oil in a wide, deep-sided, ovenproof sauté pan set over medium heat. Season the halibut with salt and pepper. Add it to the pan, skin side up, and sear it until golden brown, 4 to 5 minutes. Turn the fish, remove the pan from the heat, and use a spoon to top each fillet with some of the softened butter. Put the pan in the oven and roast just until the fish is cooked through, 2 to 3 minutes.

To serve, use a spatula to transfer the fillets to a warmed serving platter. Spoon any melted butter left in the pan over and around the fish.

PAIRINGS

Orecchiette with Shell Beans, Prosciutto, and Parmigiano-Reggiano (page 115), Cauliflower Braised with Wine, Tomatoes, and Olives (page 189)

VARIATIONS

Use the butter to top other white-fleshed fish and vegetables such as asparagus, broccoli rabe, or spinach.

FLAVOR BUILDING

You can add toasted, slivered almonds or herbs such as tarragon, chive, basil, or mint to the butter.

ROASTED MONKFISH WITH GREEN PEPPERCORN SAUCE

Monkfish belongs to a small group of fish that have little in common except for the fact that they are often cooked in ways usually reserved for beef and other meats. Tuna and swordfish are other members of this oceanic fraternity, a point emphasized by the fact that they are both purchased in portions called steaks. Because of its unusual shape, monkfish is purchased in cuts called loins. Like swordfish, it is often roasted on its uncommonly thick center bone.

Here monkfish is wrapped with bacon, seared, and set aside to let its juices redistribute—a meatlike preparation. A green peppercorn pan sauce is fashioned from the *fonds* (flavorful bits stuck to the pan), and the fish drippings are added at the last second to unite the flavors of the dish. SERVES 4

---

8 ounces thinly sliced bacon (8 slices)

1½ pounds monkfish, cut into 4 pieces

Coarse salt

Freshly ground white pepper

1 tablespoon canola oil

1 tablespoon minced shallots

1 tablespoon green peppercorns packed in brine, rinsed and finely chopped

¼ cup dry white wine

½ cup Chicken Stock (page 31)

2 tablespoons cold unsalted butter, cut into small cubes

2 tablespoons finely chopped chives

Lay 2 of the bacon slices in an overlapping pattern on your work surface, with a short edge facing you. Place one piece of monkfish crosswise along the edge closest to you, and roll the monkfish up firmly in the bacon. Season the bundle with salt and pepper, and set it aside. Repeat with the remaining bacon and monkfish.

Warm the canola oil in a wide, deep sauté pan set over medium-high heat. Add the fish bundles, seam side down, and cook for 3 to 4 minutes, until the bacon is browned and the seam is well seared and sealed. Rotate the fish a quarter-turn and cook for 2 minutes. Continue to turn and cook until browned all over, 8 to 10 minutes in all. Remove the fish bundles to a plate and cover it loosely with foil to keep them warm.

Pour off all but 2 tablespoons fat in the pan. Add the shallots and peppercorns, and sauté, stirring, for 1 minute. Pour in the wine, raise the heat to high, bring the wine to a boil, and let it reduce for 2 minutes. Pour in the stock, bring it to a boil, and let it reduce to half its volume, about 2 minutes.

Transfer the monkfish to a cutting board. Pour any juice that has accumulated around them into the sauce. Remove the pan from the heat and whisk in the butter, a piece at a time. Season the sauce with salt and swirl in the chives.

To serve, carve the monkfish crosswise into thick medallions.

Divide the medallions among four warmed dinner plates or wide, shallow bowls, and spoon the sauce over and around the fish.

PAIRING

Creamed Spinach Custards with Extra Virgin Olive Oil and Parmesan Cheese (page 197)

VARIATION

The white wine can be replaced with red.

FLAVOR BUILDING

Sauté some sliced cremini mushrooms, minced shallots, and garlic in butter and spoon over each serving.

SALMON WITH RED WINE
AND BALSAMIC VINEGAR

Because salmon is full-flavored enough to stand up to red wine, I've paired it here with a *beurre rouge*, a creamy red wine sauce that's finished by swirling in butter, enriching the sauce and giving it a silken, shiny finish. Cracked black pepper and balsamic vinegar work together to balance the sauce. SERVES 4

2 tablespoons extra virgin olive oil

2 tablespoons minced shallots

½ teaspoon cracked black pepper

1 thyme sprig

¼ cup balsamic vinegar

2 cups full-bodied red wine

2 tablespoons heavy cream

4 tablespoons (½ stick) unsalted butter, cut into 4 pieces

Coarse salt

Freshly ground white pepper

4 skinless salmon fillets
(7 ounces each)

Heat 1 tablespoon of the olive oil in a wide, deep sauté pan set over medium-high heat. Add the shallots, cracked black pepper, and thyme, and sauté for 4 minutes. Add the vinegar and wine, raise the heat to high, bring to a boil, and let reduce until just a few tablespoons remain, approximately 10 minutes. Remove the pan from the heat and whisk in the cream. Then whisk in the butter, 1 piece at a time. Pour the sauce through a fine-mesh sieve set over a bowl. Discard the solids. Season the sauce with salt and white pepper, and set it aside, covered, to keep warm.

Warm the remaining 1 tablespoon oil in a wide sauté pan set over medium-high heat. Season the salmon on both sides with salt and white pepper. Add the salmon to the pan, skinned side up, and cook until lightly browned, about 4 minutes. Turn the fillets over, lower the heat to medium, and cook for another 4 minutes.

To serve, arrange the fillets on a warmed serving platter and drizzle some sauce over each fillet. Pass the remaining sauce alongside in a sauceboat.

PAIRINGS

Roasted Tomato Risotto (page 134), Potato Puree (page 212), Wild Rice with Mushrooms, Cranberries, and Walnut Oil (page 203)

VARIATIONS

Tuna, striped bass, and monkfish are good alternatives to the salmon.

FLAVOR BUILDING

To add an aromatic component, finish each serving with chopped flat-leaf parsley, chives, tarragon, or basil.

SEARED ATLANTIC SALMON WITH WILTED ARUGULA AND HORSERADISH

One universally appreciated principle of Scandinavian cuisine is the affinity among salmon, horseradish, and dill. This dish brings those three ingredients together by fashioning a cold sour-cream-based sauce to accompany the fish, with contrast offered by the clean, peppery arugula and the lemon juice that dresses it. Be sure the oil is hot before searing the salmon; because of its fat content, this is the best way to ensure a crisp exterior without overcooking the flesh. And mound the salmon fillets on top of the arugula as soon as they're cooked so their heat wilts the greens.
SERVES 4

½ cup prepared hot horseradish

½ cup sour cream

¾ teaspoon ground caraway seeds

¼ cup chopped dill leaves

2 tablespoons very thinly sliced scallions, white and light green parts only

¼ teaspoon freshly ground black pepper

¾ teaspoon coarse salt, plus more to taste

4 cups (loosely packed) arugula leaves

1 tablespoon freshly squeezed lemon juice

2 tablespoons extra virgin olive oil

Freshly ground white pepper

1 tablespoon canola oil

4 skinless salmon fillets, approximately 1 inch think (7 ounces each)

In a small bowl, stir together the horseradish, sour cream, caraway seed, dill, scallions, black pepper, and ¾ teaspoon salt. Transfer this sauce to a sauceboat with a spoon, and set aside.

In a large bowl, toss the arugula with the lemon juice and olive oil. Season to taste with salt and white pepper. Mound the arugula in the center of a large serving plate or platter. Set aside.

Heat the canola oil in a wide sauté pan set over medium-high heat. Season the salmon fillets on both sides with salt and white pepper, and add them to the pan, skin side up. Cook until crisped and brown, about 4 minutes. Then turn them over and lower the heat to medium. Cook for an additional 3 to 4 minutes, depending on the thickness of the fish. Ideally, the salmon should be a little underdone at the center.

Arrange the salmon fillets on top of the arugula and immediately present the platter at the table, passing the horseradish sauce on the side.

VARIATIONS

Crème fraîche would be a refined alternative to the sour cream.

The salmon can be replaced by coho salmon or salmon trout.

FLAVOR BUILDING

Grill the salmon over a charcoal fire.

Add a variety of herbs, such as tarragon, parsley, and/or basil, to the sauce.

GRILLED SWORDFISH WITH SUMMER VEGETABLE COMPOTE

Swordfish is a popular catch on Long Island, where my family and I spend a fair amount of time each summer. We sometimes grill swordfish and pair it with whatever summer vegetables look most appealing at the local farm stands. Here, the fish is accompanied by a Provençal compote of olives, roasted peppers, lemon juice, and extra virgin olive oil. Using a mix of red and yellow tomatoes makes the compote especially colorful. If heirloom tomatoes are available to you, even better: Select a variety of colors and flavors, and chop them before tossing them in. SERVES 4

1 tablespoon pitted and finely chopped Niçoise olives

1 cup halved red and yellow cherry tomatoes

1 red bell pepper, roasted (page 92), peeled, and cut into small dice (½ cup diced)

2 tablespoons thinly sliced scallions (white parts only, sliced on the diagonal)

3 tablespoons extra virgin olive oil

2 teaspoons freshly squeezed lemon juice, plus more if needed

Canola oil, for brushing the fish

Coarse salt

Freshly ground black pepper

4 swordfish steaks (7 ounces each)

3 or 4 basil leaves, cut into a chiffonade

In a bowl, stir together the olives, tomatoes, diced bell pepper, and scallions. Gently stir in the olive oil and lemon juice, and season with salt and pepper. Set aside for 20 to 30 minutes at room temperature to let marinate and give the flavors a chance to develop.

Prepare an outdoor grill, letting the coals burn until they are covered with white ash.

Brush the swordfish steaks with canola oil, and season both sides with salt and pepper. Grill over medium-high heat until just cooked, about 3 minutes per side for 1-inch-thick steaks.

Stir the basil into the compote. Taste and adjust the flavors, adding a little more lemon juice and/or extra virgin olive oil if desired.

To serve, place a swordfish steak in the center of each of four warmed dinner plates and mound some compote over the fish, making sure to get a good mix of tomatoes in every serving. Spoon some of the compote's juice around each serving, and pass any extra compote on the side.

VARIATIONS

Wild striped bass, black sea bass, salmon, and tuna would all be good replacements for the swordfish in this context.

FLAVOR BUILDING

This compote practically begs you to add other ingredients, such as minced garlic and red onion, Basil Pesto (page 110), lemon oil, or even a few drops of balsamic vinegar. Chopped anchovies would help punch up its flavors as well.

CHICKEN BREASTS MARINATED WITH LEMON, SAGE, AND AGED BALSAMIC VINEGAR

Fashioning a pan sauce from a marinade is a simple technique. Here it's especially effective because pairing the pronounced sweetness of aged balsamic vinegar with lemon zest produces a bright marriage of flavors with very few ingredients. Cook the chicken slowly, as indicated; high heat will cause the sugars in the vinegar to caramelize too quickly. SERVES 4

4 tablespoons extra virgin olive oil

4 garlic cloves, peeled and thinly sliced

4 shallots, peeled and thinly sliced

¼ cup plus 3 tablespoons aged balsamic vinegar

1 teaspoon chopped rosemary

8 sage leaves, cut into a chiffonade

8 strips lemon zest, removed with a vegetable peeler and julienned

Freshly ground white pepper

4 large boneless, skinless chicken breasts (about 10 ounces each)

Coarse salt

1½ cups Chicken Stock (page 31)

2 tablespoons unsalted butter

In a container that is large enough to hold the chicken, stir together 2 tablespoons of the olive oil, the garlic, shallots, ¼ cup balsamic vinegar, rosemary, sage, and lemon zest. Season the mixture generously with pepper. Add the chicken breasts and turn them in the marinade, making sure they are well coated on both sides. Cover and refrigerate for 6 hours or overnight, turning the chicken once or twice during that time.

Remove the chicken from the container and shake off any excess marinade. Season the breasts with salt.

Strain the marinade through a small sieve set over a bowl, pressing on the solids to extract as much liquid as possible. Reserve the solids and liquid separately.

Heat the remaining 2 tablespoons oil in a wide, deep sauté pan set over medium-low heat. Add the chicken breasts to the pan and cook slowly, turning often, until nicely browned, about 12 minutes. Remove the breasts from the pan and cover them loosely with foil to keep them warm.

Add the reserved solids from the marinade to the pan and cook, stirring, for about 4 minutes. Deglaze with the marinade liquid and the remaining 3 tablespoons vinegar, and cook until the vinegar evaporates, approximately 1 minute. Add the stock, raise the heat to high, bring it to a boil, and reduce until it becomes richly flavored and lightly thickened to a sauce consistency, 3 to 4 minutes. Taste, and season with salt and pepper. Remove the pan from the heat and

swirl in the butter. Strain the sauce through a fine-mesh sieve set over a bowl, and discard the solids.

Place a chicken breast on each of four warmed dinner plates. Spoon the sauce over and around the chicken.

PAIRINGS

Whole Wheat Spaghetti, Sautéed Radicchio, Garlic, and Parmigiano-Reggiano (page 111), Pan-Roasted Zucchini with Cilantro-Mint Gremolata (page 200)

VARIATIONS

Duck breast, pheasant, quail, poussin, and—best of all—squab would all be excellent alternatives to the chicken.

FLAVOR BUILDING

Deglazing with 2 tablespoons aged sherry vinegar, rather than the balsamic vinegar, will produce a different but comparable effect.

Take this dish in a different direction by adding 6 crushed garlic cloves, a sprig of rosemary, and a few sprigs of thyme to the pan along with the chicken.

SAUTÉED CHICKEN BREASTS WITH BUTTON MUSHROOMS AND SAGE

Button mushrooms are one of those ingredients at which "serious" home cooks, and many professional chefs, turn their noses up. But the truth of the matter is that everyday button mushrooms, used the right way, can be turned into something memorable. In this quick-cooking recipe, they prove to be the perfect complement to sautéed chicken breasts, thyme, and sage. SERVES 4

4 tablespoons extra virgin olive oil

4 skinless, boneless chicken breasts (about 2 pounds total)

Coarse salt

Freshly ground white pepper

2 cups button mushrooms, sliced as thinly as possible

1 tablespoon thyme leaves

2 tablespoons chopped sage leaves

¾ cup Chicken Stock (page 31)

Preheat the oven to 375°F.

Heat 1 tablespoon of the olive oil in a wide, deep sauté pan set over medium-low heat. Season the chicken breasts with salt and pepper, add them to the pan without crowding, and cook them for 4 minutes on one side.

Meanwhile, heat 1 tablespoon of the olive oil in a separate sauté pan set over high heat. Add the mushrooms to the pan and season them with salt and pepper. Cook, stirring occasionally, until they begin to soften, 3 to 4 minutes.

Turn the chicken breasts over and scatter the thyme and sage over them. Slide the pan off the heat. Use a slotted spoon to carefully mound an equal portion of mushrooms over each chicken breast. Return the pan to the heat. Pour the stock around the breasts, and bring to a boil. Cover the pan with a domed lid or foil, and cook for 5 minutes. Use a spatula to carefully remove the chicken breasts, keeping the mushrooms neatly piled on top of each one. Set aside, covered, to keep warm.

Return the pan to the stovetop, raise the heat to high, and reduce

the liquid until lightly thickened and richly flavored, 3 to 4 minutes. Remove the pan from heat, whisk in the remaining 2 tablespoons olive oil to add body and flavor, and season to taste with salt and pepper.

Place a chicken breast with its mushrooms in the center of each of four warmed dinner plates, and carefully spoon some sauce over the top.

PAIRINGS

Sautéed Shell Beans with Pancetta (page 204), Potato Puree (page 212)

VARIATIONS

Using another type of mushroom, or a variety of mushrooms, will only make this dish more interesting. Portobellos, creminis, and chanterelles are prime candidates.

FLAVOR BUILDING

Using a few tablespoons of butter in place of the olive oil will yield a richer result.

Drizzling some white truffle oil over each serving is a perfect way to pique the mushroom flavor.

CHICKEN BRAISED WITH MORELS, LEEKS, AND RED BLISS POTATOES

My mother made a dish similar to this one with diced potatoes, celery, carrots, and rosemary, mashing the vegetables and serving the resulting sauce over pasta as a first course and following it with the chicken. Take a similar tack, tossing the vegetables and broth with pasta and serving the chicken as the main course or serve everything as one dish.

SERVES 4

1 large chicken, 4½ pounds, quartered, skin removed, cut into 8 pieces

Coarse salt and freshly ground white pepper to taste

2 tablespoons extra virgin olive oil

3 medium leeks, white parts only, thickly sliced crosswise, well washed and drained

¼ cup celery, peeled and cut into medium dice

½ cup onion, medium dice

¼ medium carrot, peeled and cut into medium dice

2 ounces dried morels or porcini, reconstituted in 1 cup hot water, drained, rinsed, and halved lengthwise

4 garlic cloves, peeled and left whole

1 sprig thyme

1 teaspoon marjoram leaves

1 sprig rosemary

3 cups Chicken Stock (page 31)

1 bay leaf

10 red bliss potatoes, halved

Season the chicken pieces with salt and pepper and let stand for 20 minutes.

Preheat the oven to 325°F.

Heat the extra virgin olive oil in a pot set over medium-high heat. Add the leeks, celery, onion, potatoes, and carrot, and cook, stirring occasionally, for 6 minutes. Season with salt and pepper. Add the morels, garlic, thyme, marjoram, and rosemary, and cook for 4 minutes more.

Add the chicken pieces, stock, and bay leaf. Raise the heat to high and bring the stock to a boil. Tightly cover the pot with a lid or aluminum foil and then place in the oven. Cook gently for 45 minutes, checking the liquid after every 15 minutes to be sure it is just barely simmering. If it's bubbling aggressively, lower the temperature by 25°. Remove the pot from the oven, remove the breast pieces and set them aside, return the pot to the oven, and cook the legs for another 10 minutes. Remove the pot from the oven and transfer the chicken pieces and potatoes to a serving platter and keep covered and warm. Let the sauce rest for 5 minutes, then skim off any fat that rises to the surface.

Use a slotted spoon to remove the garlic from the pot. Remove and discard the bay leaf and rosemary. Mash the cloves and stir them back into the liquid. Return the pot to the stove over high heat, bring the liquid to a boil, and continue to cook until reduced to 1½ cups, 15 to 20 minutes, to thicken and concentrate the flavors.

If desired, strain the sauce and spoon over the chicken, passing any extra sauce alongside in a sauceboat.

PAIRING

Shrimp Risotto with Sweet Peas, Leeks, and Chervil (page 133)

FLAVOR BUILDING

Turnips, cut into 1-inch dice, would be a great, sweet addition to the vegetables here, as would ½ cup diced fresh mushrooms and/or ½ cup chopped fresh tomatoes drained of their liquid.

CHICKEN WITH OLIVES AND PRESERVED LEMON SAUCE

The classic Moroccan tagine—a Moroccan stew cooked in a clay pot, also called a tagine—of chicken with olives and preserved lemon was a dish I had known about for years, but I didn't fully appreciate its central place in that country's cuisine until my family and I visited Morocco. There I learned that it was omnipresent, served at all classes of restaurants as well as in private homes. Despite the fact that it was enjoyed everywhere, it never lost its ability to please, in part because of the little adjustments that each chef, or home cook, makes to his own version. In fact, it was the centerpiece of one of the most enchanting restaurant experiences I've ever had, at La Maison Bleu in Fez, where my daughter Olympia and I each ordered it. In particular, I was impressed at how a modicum of ingredients can lead to such a full-flavored result.

My version of this dish weaves in elements of a traditional Moroccan marinade that is used to enliven vegetables, fish, and chicken. It has many ingredients in common with those in a tagine, not least of which is the use of both fresh and preserved lemon. But it is also flavored with cilantro and parsley, which I have added for the herbaceous lift they bring to the finished dish. SERVES 4 TO 6

2 chickens (3½ pounds each), skinned and quartered

½ cup olive oil

1 teaspoon ground ginger

1 teaspoon sweet paprika

½ teaspoon ground cumin

½ teaspoon freshly ground black pepper

½ teaspoon saffron threads

½ teaspoon ground turmeric, or an additional ½ teaspoon saffron threads

6 garlic cloves, peeled and thinly sliced

1 cup grated onion, drained

2 preserved lemons (page 15), pulp removed and set aside, peel julienned

½ cup chopped flat-leaf parsley

½ cup chopped cilantro leaves

Coarse salt

Juice of 2 lemons

1 cup pitted and halved green Moroccan olives

Harissa, optional

Put the chicken pieces in a deep baking dish that is large enough to hold them in a single layer.

Pour the oil into a small bowl. Add the ginger, paprika, cumin, pepper, saffron, turmeric, garlic, half the grated onion, and the preserved lemon pulp. Stir, pour over the chicken, cover, and marinate in the refrigerator for at least 6 hours or overnight.

Put the chicken in a large, heavy-bottomed pot with a lid. Add the remaining grated onion, ¼ cup of the parsley, ¼ cup of the cilantro, 2 cups cold water, and a pinch of salt. Bring to a boil over high heat, then cover, reduce the heat, and simmer very gently until the chicken is tender, 30 to 40 minutes.

Use a slotted spoon to transfer the chicken pieces to a warmed platter and set them aside, covered to keep them warm.

Let the cooking liquid sit for 5 minutes; then skim off any fat that has risen to the surface. Strain the cooking liquid through a fine-mesh sieve set over a bowl. Return the liquid to the pot and bring to a boil over high heat. Continue to boil until reduced to 1½ cups, 5 to 10 minutes. Add the lemon juice, olives, and preserved lemon peel. Warm through, and spoon the sauce over the chicken.

Serve the chicken from the platter, garnished with the remaining parsley, cilantro, and, if desired, harissa.

ROAST DUCK CHINOIS

One of my all-time favorite dishes is Peking duck, which I've always wanted to be able to cook at home. Unfortunately, there's no way to short-cut the traditional method, which involves days of air drying and an elaborate cooking technique that would be nearly impossible, even for a professional chef, in a home environment. Nonetheless, the recipe presented here captures one of my favorite aspects of Peking duck—the crisp, crackling skin—by pan-roasting it, then slowly roasting it in the oven and coating it with a ginger-soy-honey glaze. A host of classic Chinese flavors are combined in a paste that seasons the inside of the duck and forms the basis of an intensely complex sauce. SERVES 4

4 teaspoons rice wine vinegar

¼ cup soy sauce

¼ cup honey

1 teaspoon minced garlic, plus 4 garlic cloves, peeled and thinly sliced

2 teaspoons grated ginger, plus ¼ cup thinly sliced ginger

2 teaspoons Chinese five-spice powder

6 scallions, white parts only, thickly sliced

6 cilantro sprigs

1½ teaspoons coarse salt, plus more to taste

¼ teaspoon freshly ground black pepper, plus more to taste

¼ teaspoon ground Szechuan peppercorns

1 Long Island (Pekin) duckling (4 pounds), trimmed of excess fat, inside and outside rinsed and dried

1 tablespoon canola oil

Put the vinegar, soy sauce, honey, minced garlic, grated ginger, 1 tablespoon hot water, and 1 teaspoon of the five-spice powder in a bowl and stir them together. Set aside.

Preheat the oven to 450°F.

In a stainless steel bowl, stir together the scallions, sliced garlic, sliced ginger, cilantro, the 1½ teaspoons salt and ¼ teaspoon pepper, the remaining ½ teaspoon of the five-spice powder, and the Szechuan peppercorns. Crush the ingredients with the back of a spoon to release and further combine their flavors.

Stuff the inside of the duck with this mixture and tie the legs together with kitchen string. Season the outside of the duck with salt and pepper and the remaining ½ teaspoon five-spice powder.

Heat the canola oil in a heavy-bottomed or cast-iron pan set over very high heat. Put the duck on its side in the pan and brown it for 8 minutes. Lower the heat to medium-high, turn the duck over on its other side, and brown for 8 minutes. Turn the duck breast-side down and brown for 8 minutes. Finally, turn the duck on its back and brown for 8 minutes.

Set a rack in a roasting pan and put the duck on the rack, breast side up. Roast the duck in the oven for 40 minutes. Reduce the heat to 375°F and open the oven door for 2 minutes to allow the excess heat to escape. Cook the duck for another 45 minutes, brushing it with the glaze often during the final 20 minutes of cooking and turning the roasting pan a quarter turn each time you baste it to help the skin develop an even, deep mahogany color.

Transfer the duck to a large warmed platter and cover it loosely with foil to keep it warm. Pour the contents of the roasting pan into a small bowl. Allow the fat to rise to the surface; then skim and discard it. Strain the liquid into another bowl and discard the solids. After 10 minutes, swirl the juice that has collected in the duck's cavity into the sauce.

Carve the duck and serve it from a platter, passing the sauce alongside.

PAIRING

Sautéed Spinach with Garlic, Ginger, and Sesame Oil (page 199)

DUCK VINDALOO

One of my favorite take-out dishes from the Indian restaurants in our neighborhood is lamb vindaloo, which inspired this recipe. I thought this was a unique variation, but I have subsequently learned that duck vindaloo is a specialty of Goa, a state in southwestern India. The sauce will register as very spicy when tasted alone, but when spooned over the bird, it will seem much less intense. The combination of Sri Lankan chili powder and fresh chile pepper is very spicy; feel free to substitute others if you have a low threshold for heat. SERVES 4 TO 6

⅔ cup white wine vinegar

¼ cup grapeseed oil

6 garlic cloves, peeled and finely chopped

1 tablespoon finely chopped jalapeño pepper, seeds removed

1½ cups diced onions (½-inch dice)

1 tablespoon minced ginger

¼ cup curry powder

1 teaspoon Sri Lankan hot chili powder, or ½ teaspoon cayenne pepper

2 Muscovy or Pekin ducks, quartered, bone-in, breasts and legs trimmed and scored (ask your butcher to do this)

2 tablespoons canola oil

¼ cup whole canned tomatoes, drained and chopped

3 cups Chicken Stock (page 31), plus ½ cup stock or water for deglazing

Coarse salt

Freshly ground black pepper to taste

¼ cup chopped cilantro leaves

¼ cup thinly sliced scallions, white part only

In a baking dish, stir together the vinegar, grapeseed oil, garlic, jalapeño, onions, ginger, curry powder, and chili powder. Add the duck, turn the pieces to coat them with the sauce, cover, and marinate in the refrigerator overnight.

Preheat the oven to 400°F.

Remove the duck pieces from the marinade, shaking off any excess marinade, and set them aside. Strain the marinade through a fine-mesh sieve set over a bowl. Reserve the solids and liquid separately.

Heat 1 tablespoon of the canola oil in a sauté pan set over medium-high heat. Add the marinade solids and cook for 7 minutes, stirring often, until lightly browned and fragrant. Add the reserved marinade liquid, tomatoes, and the 3 cups stock. Bring to a boil over high heat, and continue to boil until reduced by half, about 30 minutes. During this time, the sauce will thicken and become pleasingly hot and spicy.

Meanwhile, season the duck pieces with salt and pepper. Heat the remaining 1 tablespoon oil in an ovenproof sauté pan over high heat. Add the duck pieces, skin side down, and brown them, about 8 minutes. Drain any excess fat from the pan. Turn the pieces over and place the sauté pan in the oven. Roast for 12 to 14 minutes for a medium-rare duck breast. Remove the duck breasts to a warmed platter, leaving the other pieces in the oven for another 4 minutes. Transfer the remaining duck pieces to the platter and cover them with foil to keep them warm. Add the ½ cup stock to the pan, and scrape the bottom of the pan to loosen any flavorful bits and incorporate them. Then swirl this mixture into the sauce in the other pan.

Remove the foil from the platter and pour any juices that have collected into the sauce. Spoon the sauce over the duck. Garnish with a shower of cilantro and scallions, and serve, passing any extra sauce alongside in a sauceboat.

PAIRING

Curried Cauliflower with Scallions and Golden Raisins (page 190)

PAN-ROASTED SQUAB WITH BUTTER-BRAISED SAVOY CABBAGE AND GREEN APPLES

Sometimes just a few components are all that's required to make a meal compelling and satisfying. For example, cabbage, apples, and squab are made for each other, and here they come together in a dish that's perfect for winter, thanks to the richness of the squab and butter and the treatment of the cabbage, which recalls Alsatian cuisine. SERVES 4

4 whole squabs (about 18 ounces each)

4 tablespoons (½ stick) unsalted butter

1 large head Savoy cabbage, quartered, cored, and sliced crosswise into ½-inch strips (about 8 cups sliced)

Coarse salt to taste

Freshly ground black pepper to taste

½ teaspoon ground caraway seeds

2 Granny Smith apples, peeled, cored, and cut into ¼-inch dice (3 cups diced)

1 tablespoon olive oil

Using a sharp knife, cut the wing tips off the squabs. Cut down each side of the backbones, and remove the bones. Put the squabs, breast side up, on your work surface. Press down on the breast with the heel of your hand to crack the breast keel bone. Turn the squabs over and pull out the keel bone. Cut each squab in half and set aside.

Melt 3 tablespoons of the butter in a large sauté pan set over medium-low heat. Add the cabbage, salt, pepper, and caraway, and cook, stirring occasionally, until the cabbage is tender, about 15 minutes. Stir in the diced apple and continue cooking for 5 more minutes. The cabbage should be tender but still firm. Remove the pan from the heat and stir in the remaining 1 tablespoon butter. Season to taste with salt and pepper, and transfer the cabbage to a warm serving platter. Cover it with foil to keep it warm.

Heat the olive oil in an ovenproof sauté pan set over medium heat. Season the squab pieces with salt and pepper, and add them to the pan, skin side down. Cook slowly, allowing the fat to render gradually,

until the skin is nicely browned, approximately 6 minutes. Turn the pieces over and continue cooking, basting occasionally, for 4 minutes for medium-rare. Remove the pan from the heat and cover the squab with foil to keep it warm.

Divide the cabbage among four warmed dinner plates, mounding it in the center. Arrange 2 squab halves atop each mound, and pour any collected juices over the squab.

PAIRING
Oven-Roasted Mushrooms (page 210)

VARIATION
Duck breast would be an ideal alternative to the squab.

FLAVOR BUILDING
Roasted root vegetables have a natural affinity for game, so serve this with diced parsnips, carrots, and/or turnips.

BRAISED PORK WITH FENNEL
AND RED BLISS POTATOES

When I worked with the French chef Michel Guérard, we made a version of this dish with rack of veal. This recipe uses pork, which I prefer. Roasting the meat and vegetables together in a small quantity of rich chicken stock yields a generous amount of herbaceous sauce, as well as meltingly tender fennel and potatoes—a complete meal with very little work. SERVES 4

3 tablespoons olive oil

2½ pounds boneless pork loin, tied by your butcher

Coarse salt

Cracked white pepper

2 teaspoons fennel seeds, toasted

1 fennel bulb, stems attached, halved lengthwise and cut into thick wedges

1 large onion, peeled and quartered with the root end attached

⅓ cup diced peeled celery (small dice)

8 garlic cloves, peeled

⅓ cup diced carrot (small dice)

½ cup dry white wine

¾ cup canned whole tomatoes, drained

12 small Red Bliss potatoes

2 rosemary sprigs

3 thyme sprigs

1 bay leaf, crumbled

2½ cups Chicken Stock (page 31)

Preheat the oven to 325°F.

Heat 2 tablespoons of the olive oil in a roasting pan set over medium-high heat. Season the pork generously with salt, pepper, and the fennel seeds. Add the pork to the pan and brown on all sides, about 10 minutes. Remove and set aside.

Add the remaining 1 tablespoon oil, the fennel wedges, and the onion quarters to the pan, and brown, turning, for 6 minutes. Add the celery, garlic, and carrots, and cook for 2 more minutes. Deglaze with the wine, scraping up any flavorful bits stuck on the bottom of the pan, and continue to cook until the wine is reduced by half, 2 to 3 minutes.

Return the pork to the pan. Add the tomatoes, potatoes, rosemary, thyme, bay leaf, and stock. Bring the liquid to a boil over high heat; then lower the heat until the liquid is just simmering. Loosely cover the pan with foil and transfer it to the oven. Cook for 1 hour and 40 minutes, or until the pork's internal temperature reaches 155°F. Check the roast after 15 minutes, and again periodically to be sure that the braising liquid is barely simmering; adjust the oven temperature if necessary to maintain a gentle simmer.

When the pork is done, use tongs and/or a slotted spoon to remove the meat to a cutting board and the vegetables to a plate or bowl. Transfer the liquid to a saucepan and let it rest for 5 minutes; then skim off any fat that has risen to the surface. Set the pan over high heat, bring the liquid to a boil, and continue to boil until reduced to 1¼ cups, about 10 minutes.

Meanwhile, slice the roast and arrange it in the center of a warmed serving platter. Arrange the potatoes and fennel decoratively around it, and cover the platter with foil if necessary to keep the meat and vegetables warm. When the sauce has reduced, strain it. Taste, and adjust the seasoning with salt and pepper.

Serve the pork and vegetables from the platter, passing the sauce alongside in a sauceboat.

VARIATION

Loin or rib of veal can stand in for the pork here, but omit the fennel seed.

FLAVOR BUILDING

For a potent mushroom flavor, add some dried porcini or morel mushrooms to the pan along with the vegetables.

GRILLED MARINATED PORK CHOPS

During a ski vacation in a remote area of British Columbia, it was my turn to cook dinner for our family and traveling companions. While I usually enjoy the opportunity to cook for those closest to me, especially in such a relaxed setting, this was a challenge because the offerings at the local supermarket were sparse. I skipped right past the seafood and selected the most appealing cut of meat from the butcher department, pork chops. Back at the house, I aggressively seasoned them with lots of chopped garlic, cracked black pepper, rosemary, thyme, and sage, drizzled them with extra virgin olive oil, and gave those elements time to seep in. When the time came to cook, I ignored the winter conditions and fired up the outdoor grill, and was it ever worth it.

This improvisation was a powerful reminder of the great results that can be attained by adhering to the classic adage about building a dish from the ground up, starting with the best meat, poultry, or fish available and making all other decisions around it. SERVES 4

---

4 pork chops, about 2 inches thick (14 ounces each), bone in

6 garlic cloves, peeled and finely chopped

1 tablespoon thyme leaves

1½ tablespoons thinly sliced sage leaves

2 large rosemary sprigs, chopped, plus 4 small sprigs for optional garnish

2 teaspoons black peppercorns, coarsely cracked

3 tablespoons extra virgin olive oil

Coarse salt

Put the pork chops in a shallow dish that is wide enough to hold them in a single layer. Add the garlic, thyme, sage, rosemary, peppercorns, and olive oil. Turn the chops over in the oil and herbs until they are thoroughly and evenly coated. Cover and refrigerate for at least 2 hours or overnight. (The longer they marinate, the more flavorful they will become.)

When you are ready to cook, prepare an outdoor grill, letting the coals burn until they are covered with white ash.

Remove the chops from the bowl, and brush off any excess marinade. Season them generously with salt. Grill over medium-hot coals, turning once, until pink at the bone, 20 to 25 minutes, or 12 to15 minutes per inch of thickness.

Transfer the chops to a warmed serving platter or individual plates. Garnish with rosemary sprigs if desired, and serve at once.

PAIRINGS

Spaghetti with Hot and Sweet Peppers (page 130), Wild Rice with Mushrooms, Cranberries, and Walnut Oil (page 203), Escarole, White Beans, and Apple-Smoked Bacon (page 194)

VARIATION

For an indoor variation of this dish, slowly pan-roast the pork, then deglaze with red wine over medium-low heat to make a pan sauce.

FILET MIGNON WITH MADEIRA SAUCE

When I worked for the Troisgros brothers at their restaurant in France in the early 1980s, we made côte de boeuf by slowly pan-roasting it in a high-sided pot where it was continuously basted to form a thick, flavorful crust. Here I add rosemary and thyme sprigs, allowing the herbs to infuse the butter as it bastes the meat so their flavors get subtly passed along. SERVES 4

4 center-cut filet mignons,
2½ inches thick (10 ounces each)

Coarse salt

Freshly cracked black pepper

2 tablespoons canola oil

4 tablespoons (½ stick) unsalted butter

1 thyme sprig

1 rosemary sprig

2 tablespoons minced shallots

¼ cup Madeira

2 cups Chicken Stock (page 31) or store-bought or homemade veal stock

1 tablespoon Dijon mustard

Remove the filets from the refrigerator 30 minutes before cooking, and season them all over with salt and pepper.

Warm the canola oil in a heavy-bottomed sauté pan set over medium-high heat. Add the filets and sear well on both sides, 3 to 4 minutes per side.

When all sides of the filets are brown, add 2 tablespoons of the butter and the rosemary and thyme sprigs to the pan, and reduce the heat to medium-low. Baste the steaks continually with melted butter while they cook, taking care not to let the butter brown. Cook for approximately 14 minutes for rare, 18 minutes for medium-rare, and 20 minutes for medium, depending on the thickness of the filets. When the beef is done, transfer the filets to a plate and cover them loosely with foil to keep them warm.

Pour off all but 2 tablespoons of the fat from the pan. Add the shallots and cook for 2 minutes. Then add the Madeira and cook, scraping up any flavorful bits that are stuck to the bottom of the pan. Add the stock, raise the heat to high, and cook until reduced by three-quarters, or until lightly thickened

and nicely flavored, 12 to 15 minutes.

Strain the sauce through a fine-mesh sieve set over a bowl. Return it to the pan over medium-low heat, and whisk in the mustard, then the remaining 2 tablespoons butter, 1 piece at a time. Season to taste with salt and pepper.

Place each filet in the center of a warmed dinner plate, and spoon some sauce over each serving.

PAIRINGS

Tagliatelle with Squid, Scallops, and Shrimp (page 112), Creamed Spinach Custards with Extra Virgin Olive Oil and Parmesan Cheese (page 197), Oven-Roasted Mushrooms (page 210)

VARIATIONS

The Madeira sauce is a versatile one to add to your repertoire. Because this fortified wine's sweet flavor, concentrated by reducing, infuses the entire sauce, using another wine or spirit alters its character substantially. My three favorite adaptations are achieved by replacing the ¼ cup Madeira with the following wines/spirits and reducing by two-thirds:

- Cognac, ¼ cup. With a higher percentage of alcohol by volume and the most complex nose of the options presented here, Cognac will produce an elegant, nuanced sauce.

- Port, ¼ cup. Port will yield a more concentrated, sweeter flavor than Madeira.

- Red wine, 1 cup. This results in a simplified bordelaise sauce. Use a full-bodied red wine. If practical, select the same wine you will be drinking with the filet.

SPICY GRILLED SKIRT STEAK

The spice rub my cooks use to make grilled skirt steak for family meal (industry-speak for staff dinner) in the Gotham kitchen is a simple blend that conjures up authentic Southwestern flavor. It boasts a pleasing balance of heat from chiles and both cayenne and black pepper, sweetness from onions, and a touch of citrus from lime juice and orange zest. SERVES 4 TO 6

¼ cup canola oil

½ cup grated onion

2 tablespoons freshly squeezed lime juice

1 teaspoon grated orange zest

2½ tablespoons finely chopped garlic

2 teaspoons finely chopped jalapeño pepper

1 tablespoon ancho chile powder

½ teaspoon cayenne pepper

1½ tablespoons coarsely ground black pepper

1 teaspoon dried oregano

2 pounds skirt steak

In a small bowl, make a paste by stirring together all of the ingredients except the steak.

Coat the steak with the marinade. Cover and refrigerate it for 6 hours or overnight.

Prepare an outdoor grill, letting the coals burn until they are covered with white ash.

Put the steak on the grate over hot coals, and grill, turning once, for a total of 4 to 5 minutes for medium-rare or 7 minutes for medium. Let rest for 10 minutes, then carve thinly across the grain. Serve from a warmed platter.

PAIRINGS

Watermelon, Cherry Tomato, Red Onion, and Cucumber Salad (page 44), Spicy Shrimp Salad with Mango, Avocado, and Lime Vinaigrette (page 54), Fennel Coleslaw (page 211).

VARIATION

This could be made just as easily with hangar steak or a whole tenderloin of beef. For the latter, grill the tenderloin, turning often, until the internal temperature is 130°F, approximately 35 minutes.

OXTAIL BRAISED IN RED WINE WITH MASHED ROOT VEGETABLES

Oxtail is one of those cuts, like lamb shanks, that depends on long, slow braising to render it meltingly tender and succulent. Like most dishes that call for such patient cooking, it's especially well suited to fall and winter weather.

Tradition dictates that braised oxtail should be served with potato puree or another starch capable of soaking up the flavorful braising liquid, which is usually reduced and used as a sauce. Here, this is achieved by cooking root vegetables along with the oxtail during the final hour of cooking. They are then mashed with butter and some of the braising liquid for a unique puree with the distinct yet balanced flavors of celery root, carrot, turnip, and parsnip. The combination, like oxtail itself, is the perfect culinary answer to the frigid weather that defines the first and last months of the year in many parts of the country. SERVES 4

---

2 tablespoons canola oil

4 pounds oxtail, trimmed of excess fat (8 to 10 large pieces), ask your butcher to trim the fat, but not the silverskin, which holds the meat onto the bone

Coarse salt

Freshly ground black pepper to taste

1 large onion, peeled and cut into large dice (about 1½ cups)

4 large garlic cloves, peeled and smashed

2 thyme sprigs

1 bay leaf

2 cups full-bodied red wine

1 cup drained, finely chopped canned whole tomatoes

3 cups Chicken Stock (page 31) or veal stock

1 head celery root, peeled and quartered

2 medium parsnips, peeled and chopped crosswise into three pieces

2 medium carrots, peeled and chopped crosswise into three pieces

3 medium turnips, peeled and quartered

1 tablespoon unsalted butter

2 tablespoons chopped chives

Preheat the oven to 325°F.

Heat the oil in an ovenproof casserole set over medium-high heat. Season the oxtail with salt and pepper, add to the casserole, and brown on all sides, 8 minutes. Remove the oxtail and set it aside.

Lower the heat, add the onion, and sauté until lightly browned, approximately 4 minutes. Add the garlic, thyme, and bay leaf, and cook for 1 minute. Add the red wine, bring to a boil over high heat, and continue to boil until reduced to a little more than ½ cup, 10 to 12 minutes. Add the tomatoes, oxtail, stock, and a pinch of salt. Bring the liquid to a boil and skim any impurities that rise to the surface.

Cover the casserole with a tight-fitting lid or seal with aluminum foil, and roast in the preheated oven for 1¼ hours. Every 15 minutes, check to be sure the liquid is just barely simmering; if bubbling too aggressively, lower the heat by 25°. Add the celery root, parsnips, carrots, and turnips, replace the cover, and cook for 1 hour more, or until the meat begins to separate from the bone and the vegetables are tender but still retain their shape.

Remove the oxtail from the pot and arrange the pieces on a platter, covered with foil to keep warm. Use a slotted spoon to transfer the vegetables and garlic cloves to a bowl. Remove the bay leaf. Reduce the remaining liquid over high heat, skimming often, for about 20 minutes, or until thickened and richly flavored. Use tongs or a slotted spoon to remove and discard the bay leaf.

Meanwhile, mash the vegetables and garlic with a potato masher together with 2 tablespoons of the reduced cooking liquid and the butter. Season the puree to taste with salt and pepper. Transfer the puree to a serving bowl and keep covered and warm.

To serve, spoon the sauce over the oxtail, garnish with a scattering of chives, and pass the mashed vegetables alongside.

PAIRING

Pan-Roasted Mushrooms, Chestnuts, and Pearl Onions (page 208)

VARIATION

Beef short ribs, easier to find than oxtail in many markets, will yield a comparable result.

ACCOMPANIMENTS AND SIDE DISHES

FOR THE MOST PART, THE RECIPES IN THIS CHAPTER begin with one central ingredient and then layer on complementary flavors. You might be surprised at how satisfying the results can be. Dishes as simple as Oven-Roasted Mushrooms or Pan-Roasted Zucchini with Cilantro-Mint Gremolata are not only fragrant and delicious, but also arrestingly beautiful. Others derive their impact from unexpected combinations or by introducing a new ingredient into a familiar context, like making coleslaw with fennel instead of cabbage. One of my personal favorites is a reimagining of creamed spinach as Creamed Spinach Custards with Extra Virgin Olive Oil and Parmesan Cheese, a versatile side dish that might just become your favorite accompaniment to steak.

Like many of the main courses with which you'll be pairing them, there are international influences here: a touch of Spain in Chickpeas, Smoked Paprika, and Cilantro and of India in Curried Cauliflower with Scallions and Golden Raisins, to name just two.

Most of these recipes are followed by a Pairing note, offering a thought or two on other dishes with which to match them. If you are looking for more ways to employ these accompaniments, it's generally best to remain culturally consistent, keeping Mediterranean, Asian, and South American dishes matched with others from the same region. But you never know; you might find inspired pairings that defy convention, and if they taste good to you, there's no reason not to engage in some culinary cross-pollination.

CHICKPEAS, SMOKED PAPRIKA, AND CILANTRO

Inspired by Middle Eastern salads, this chickpea dish owes its distinct flavor to smoked paprika, a Spanish spice (known in Spain as *pimentón de la vera*) produced via an irresistible process: Capsicum peppers are hand-harvested each October, then smoked over a smoldering oak fire for fifteen days, during which time they soak up the wood flavor while maintaining their distinct red tint. They are then stone-ground to a humble powder that looks like any other spice, but on the palate, every day of that smoking registers loud and clear. You can also make this with sweet or hot regular paprika. SERVES 4 TO 6

½ cup extra virgin olive oil

1 tablespoon finely minced garlic

½ cup thinly sliced shallot rings (from about 2 shallots)

2 cups dried chickpeas, cooked (3 cups cooked), or 3 cups canned chickpeas, drained

2 teaspoons ground cumin

2 tablespoons smoked paprika

Coarse salt

Freshly ground black pepper

¼ cup chopped cilantro leaves

Warm the olive oil in a heavy-bottomed saucepan set over medium heat. Add the garlic and cook, stirring often, until golden brown, 2 to 3 minutes. Add the shallots, chickpeas, cumin, and paprika, reduce the heat to low, and cook for 3 minutes. Season to taste with salt and pepper.

Stir in the chopped cilantro, transfer to a warmed serving bowl, and serve hot. (This can also be served at room temperature. Let the mixture cool before adding the cilantro.)

VARIATION

Scallions or Spanish onion can replace the shallots.

FLAVOR BUILDING

Add heat and texture with sliced sweet and spicy peppers, such as red bell and/or assorted chiles.

CAULIFLOWER BRAISED WITH WINE, TOMATOES, AND OLIVES

This is a Provençal take on cauliflower *à la Grecque* ("in the Greek manner"), featuring white wine, Niçoise olives, parsley, and basil. Vegetables prepared in this manner—such as mushrooms, artichokes, and cauliflower—are gently cooked in a combination of stock or water and white wine, vinegar, or lemon juice, and enhanced by the defining spice, coriander seed. The vegetables are traditionally served cold, making them a delicious convenience that actually improves after a day or two in the refrigerator.

In a twist on tradition, the cooking liquid here is reduced to concentrate the flavors, then spooned back over the cauliflower. SERVES 4

3 tablespoons extra virgin olive oil

½ cup diced onion

2 sprigs thyme

2 garlic cloves, peeled and finely chopped

1 bay leaf

½ teaspoon ground coriander seeds

1 cup drained, finely chopped canned tomatoes (about ⅓ of a 28-ounce can)

⅔ cup dry white wine

1 head cauliflower cut into florets, about 6 cups

3 cups Chicken Stock (page 31)

Coarse salt and freshly ground pepper to taste

3 tablespoons pitted, sliced Niçoise olives

1 tablespoon chopped flat-leaf parsley

2 tablespoons chopped basil

Heat 2 tablespoons of the extra virgin olive oil in a pot set over medium-high heat. Add the onion and sauté for 4 minutes. Add the thyme, garlic, bay leaf, and coriander seeds, and cook for 2 to 3 minutes more. Add the tomatoes and white wine, raise the heat to high, bring the liquid to a boil, and continue to boil and reduce for 6 minutes.

Add the cauliflower and stock to the pot and season with salt and pepper. Bring to a boil, then reduce the heat and let simmer until the cauliflower is tender, about 7 minutes. Use a slotted spoon to transfer the cauliflower to a serving platter and set it aside. Remove the bay leaf.

Raise the heat to high, return the liquid to a boil, and continue to boil to reduce and concentrate the flavors, approximately 10 minutes more. You should have about 1 cup liquid. Add the herbs and olives, taste, and adjust the seasoning if necessary. Spoon the sauce over the cauliflower and serve.

PAIRING

Roasted Halibut with Lemon-Caper Butter (page 155)

VARIATION

This recipe can be adapted for button mushrooms or fennel, cutting a large bulb into 6 to 8 pieces, leaving the core end intact.

CURRIED CAULIFLOWER WITH SCALLIONS AND GOLDEN RAISINS

In this regal side dish, the curry-tinged cauliflower appears positively golden. Because cauliflower is white inside and out, it's easy to forget that it belongs to the mustard family, but this fact may never elude you again after you taste this dish's piquant flavors. Its deceptively velvety mouthfeel owes nothing to cream or butter, but is achieved by pureeing some of the cooked cauliflower and returning it to the sauce. This versatile dish, which is as compelling cold as it is hot, is good served with basmati rice. SERVES 6

1 tablespoon canola oil

½ medium onion, peeled and chopped

3 garlic cloves, peeled and chopped

1 tablespoon Madras curry powder

1 teaspoon turmeric, optional

Pinch of red pepper flakes

4 whole canned plum tomatoes, gently crushed by hand

1 large head cauliflower (about 2 pounds), separated into large florets

2 cups Chicken Stock (page 31)

2 to 3 teaspoons lime juice

Coarse salt

Freshly ground black pepper

2 tablespoons golden raisins, plumped in hot water for 10 minutes and drained

2 scallions, white and light green parts only, sliced

1 tablespoon chopped cilantro leaves

Warm the oil over medium low heat in a saucepan that is large enough to hold all of the cauliflower without crowding. Add the onions and garlic and cook for 2 minutes. Add the curry powder, turmeric if using, red pepper flakes, and tomatoes. Stir and cook gently for 5 minutes.

Add the cauliflower and chicken stock, and season to taste with salt and pepper. Raise the heat to high and bring the liquid to a boil. Then lower the heat and simmer until the cauliflower is just cooked through, approximately 10 minutes.

Use a slotted spoon to transfer the cauliflower and tomato pieces to a warmed serving bowl, leaving 2 florets behind. Cover the bowl to keep warm. Continue to cook the florets until they are quite soft, approximately 5 more minutes. Use a hand-held blender placed directly into the pot to purée these soft florets and thicken the sauce. (Alternatively, mash them with a fork in a small bowl and return the puree to the sauce.) Add 2 teaspoons lime juice, taste, and adjust the seasoning with salt and pepper if necessary. Stir in more

lime juice, if needed, to lift the flavors.

Spoon some of the sauce over the cauliflower, and serve garnished with the raisins, scallions, and cilantro. Pass the remaining sauce on the side.

PAIRING

Duck Vindaloo (page 171)

CURRIED CREAMED CORN

While making a tour of San Francisco restaurants, I was served corn on the cob topped with a compound butter that took me several minutes to place as being flavored with curry. This recipe borrows that inspiring combination, adding garlic and chile. You can make a lighter version by omitting the cream, and it can be made ahead and served at room temperature. It's especially appropriate as an accompaniment to roasted and grilled meats. SERVES 4

6 ears corn

3 tablespoons unsalted butter

½ cup finely chopped onion

1 small jalapeño chile pepper, halved, seeded, and finely chopped (about 2½ teaspoons chopped)

2 teaspoons finely chopped garlic

2 teaspoons Madras curry powder

½ cup heavy cream

Coarse salt

Freshly ground white pepper

¼ cup chopped cilantro leaves

Trim the stalk end of 1 ear of corn to enable you to stand it on end securely. Stand the ear of corn on a cutting board and set the blade of a very sharp chef's knife at a slight angle at the top of the ear, where the kernels meet the cob. Draw the knife down along the cob, detaching the kernels. Work your way around the cob, repeating until all the kernels are removed. Repeat with the remaining ears. You should have about 4 cups of kernels.

Melt 2 tablespoons of the butter in a wide, deep sauté pan set over low heat. Add the onions and sauté for 5 minutes. Add the chile and garlic, stir, and cook for 2 more minutes. Add the curry powder, stir to coat the other ingredients, and continue cooking for 2 minutes. Add the corn, stir well, and continue cooking for 3 minutes more. Stir in the cream, season with salt and pepper, and cook until slightly thickened, 2 to 3 minutes. Stir in the remaining 1 tablespoon butter to enrich the dish. Then add the chopped cilantro.

Serve the curried creamed corn family-style from a large warmed serving bowl, or spoon it onto a dinner plate alongside any other accompaniments.

VARIATION

Leave out the heavy cream for a lighter version and a more pronounced corn flavor.

FLAVOR BUILDING

Sauté 1 diced red bell pepper along with the other vegetables and/or add ½ cup minced scallions along with the cilantro at the end.

ESCAROLE, WHITE BEANS, AND APPLE-SMOKED BACON

This dish pairs well with a wide range of foods, from roasted meats to fish. It's also a year-round component, hearty enough for winter (especially if you substitute blanched cabbage for the escarole) but also perfectly at home in summer. I often make the stirring of butter into a dish at the end of a recipe optional, but it really pulls the flavors of this one together. SERVES 4 TO 6

1 cup dried white runner beans or Great Northern beans

Coarse salt

1 large head escarole, cut into wedges with the root end intact

3 ounces apple-smoked slab bacon, in one piece

1 bay leaf

½ onion, peeled and halved

4 garlic cloves, peeled

3 cups Chicken Stock (page 31)

1 tablespoon extra virgin olive oil

Freshly ground white pepper

1 tablespoon unsalted butter

Soak the beans overnight in enough cold water to cover them by 1 inch. Drain. Or use the quick-soak method (page 30).

Bring a pot of salted water to a boil. Fill a large bowl halfway with ice water.

Cook the escarole in the boiling water for 3 minutes, then remove it with tongs and submerge it in the ice water to stop the cooking and preserve its color. Squeeze out the excess liquid, remove the core, and cut the escarole crosswise into 2-inch pieces. Set aside.

Put the beans, bacon, bay leaf, onions, garlic, and stock in a pot. Bring to a boil over high heat, then lower the heat and simmer until the beans are cooked, about 50 minutes. Use tongs to pick out and discard the bay leaf and onion.

Strain the beans in a fine-mesh sieve set over a bowl. Reserve the cooking liquid. Use tongs to pick out and set aside the bacon and garlic. When it is cool enough to handle, cut the bacon into ¼-inch dice and set aside. Mash the garlic into a paste and stir it into the strained stock. You should have approximately ½ cup of liquid. Set aside.

Heat the oil in a sauté pan set over medium-high heat. Add the escarole, season with salt and pepper, and sauté for 2 minutes. Add the beans and reserved bacon, then the reserved cooking liquid. Stir together and season. Stir in the butter to enrich the flavors.

Transfer the contents of the pan to a warmed serving bowl, and present family-style from the center of the table.

PAIRING

Grilled Marinated Pork Chops (page 176)

VARIATIONS

Savoy cabbage can take the place of the escarole.

Chickpeas are a fine substitute for the runner beans.

FLAVOR BUILDING

For a slightly spicier dish, replace the bacon with sliced chorizo and finish the dish with chopped cilantro. Or stir in 1 pound of sliced, sautéed wild or cultivated mushrooms at the end.

CREAMED SPINACH CUSTARDS WITH EXTRA VIRGIN OLIVE OIL AND PARMESAN CHEESE

When it comes to steakhouse menus, I'm a purist. I like a porterhouse steak, potatoes, and creamed spinach with lots of garlic. This recipe is a play on the latter, a silken side dish that's a versatile accompaniment not just to steak but to a variety of roasted meats and poultry. The bottom of the custard turns a beautiful, dark forest green that gets progressively lighter toward the top, where the cream shows more than the vegetable. SERVES 6

2 cups heavy cream

1 teaspoon coarse salt, plus more to taste

½ teaspoon freshly ground white pepper, plus more to taste

2 cups (tightly packed) spinach leaves

1 tablespoon Roasted Garlic Puree (recipe follows)

4 eggs, beaten

Extra virgin olive oil

Grated Parmigiano-Reggiano

Freshly ground black pepper

Preheat the oven to 325°F.

Fill a large bowl halfway with ice water.

Pour the cream into a saucepan and bring it to a boil over high heat. Immediately remove the pan from the heat, add the 1 teaspoon salt and ½ teaspoon pepper, and then add the spinach and stir until wilted. Rest the bottom of the pot in the ice water and stir the spinach to cool it as quickly as possible.

When the spinach-cream mixture is cool, whisk in the eggs. Puree the mixture with a hand mixer or in a blender. Strain it through a fine-mesh sieve set over a bowl. Taste, and correct the seasoning if necessary.

Set six buttered ramekins in a roasting pan without crowding. Divide the custard among the ramekins. Pour warm water into the pan so it reaches halfway up the sides of the ramekins. Place the pan in the oven and bake for 25 minutes. Turn the pan 180 degrees and bake for an additional 30 minutes, or until the custards are set around the edges but still a little shaky in the center.

Unmold the custards onto individual warmed plates. Drizzle with extra virgin olive oil and lightly dust with grated cheese and a few grindings of black pepper. Serve hot.

ROASTED GARLIC PUREE

20 large garlic cloves, unpeeled

1 tablespoon extra virgin olive oil

Coarse salt

Freshly ground white pepper to taste

Preheat the oven to 325°F.

Put the garlic in a small baking dish and toss with the oil and 1 tablespoon water. Season with salt and pepper. Cover with aluminum foil and bake until the garlic is tender, 25 to 35 minutes. Remove the dish from the oven, uncover, and set aside to cool.

When the garlic has cooled, squeeze the cloves out of their skin into a small bowl, and mash with a fork.

One large head of garlic will yield about 3 tablespoons puree, a sweet condiment that can be stirred into soups, risotto, and other dishes.

PAIRINGS

Filet Mignon with Madeira Sauce (page 178), Roasted Monkfish with Green Peppercorn Sauce (page 157)

VARIATION

If you don't have time to roast the garlic, use ¼ to ½ teaspoon minced fresh garlic instead of the puree.

FLAVOR BUILDING

Top each custard with sautéed thinly sliced cremini mushrooms, and serve as a first course.

SAUTÉED SPINACH WITH GARLIC, GINGER, AND SESAME OIL

If you like spinach sautéed with olive oil and garlic, you'll want to try this version, which piles on the high-impact flavors of sesame and ginger. Serve this as an accompaniment to grilled or roasted chicken and fish. SERVES 4

Coarse salt

1 tablespoon unsalted butter

8 cups (tightly packed) spinach leaves (about 1 pound)

2 tablespoons grapeseed oil or other neutral-flavored oil

1 tablespoon minced garlic

1 tablespoon plus 1 teaspoon grated ginger

1 teaspoon sesame oil

Freshly ground black pepper

Bring 3 quarts of water to a boil, season with salt, and add the butter. Add the spinach, cook until just wilted, about 20 seconds, and drain. Spread the spinach out on a mesh rack set over a cookie sheet to let it cool as quickly as possible. Then place the spinach in a clean kitchen towel and gently squeeze out the excess water. Set aside.

Put the grapeseed oil, garlic, and ginger in a large sauté pan set over medium heat. Cook, stirring constantly, for 2 minutes. Add the spinach, stir, and sauté for 1 minute or until heated through. Stir in the sesame oil. Taste, and adjust the seasoning with salt and pepper.

Transfer the spinach to a warmed serving bowl and pass it with other dishes. Or let it cool and serve cold or at room temperature.

PAIRINGS

Roast Duck Chinois (page 170), Asian Striped Bass *en Papillote* (page 142), Honey-Ginger Glazed Quail on Wilted Lettuces (page 61)

VARIATION

Bok choy or Swiss chard, cooked in the same way, would both be good alternatives to the spinach.

FLAVOR BUILDING

Add 1 tablespoon white sesame seeds to the dish at the end, toasting them briefly in the pan.

PAN-ROASTED ZUCCHINI WITH CILANTRO-MINT GREMOLATA

Most chefs enjoy the challenge of taking something ordinary and turning it into something delicious. I know I do. This recipe began with the notion of turning small zucchini—which tend to be mild in flavor—into something special. The solution began with halving and sautéing the zucchini. With their flesh exposed, salted, and browned, the zucchini are primed to receive flavor, delivered here by a mint variation on gremolata, the parsley-lemon-garlic mixture that traditionally garnishes osso buco. I've crossed gremolata with *pangriata,* an Italian bread crumb and herb mixture. This side dish is especially appropriate to summer dinners, where it makes a perfect companion to grilled fish. SERVES 6

6 slender green zucchini
(about 1 small zucchini per person),
halved lengthwise

¼ teaspoon coarse salt, plus more
to taste

3 tablespoons chopped mint leaves

3 tablespoons chopped cilantro
leaves

½ garlic clove, peeled and finely
chopped

Finely chopped zest of 1 lemon

Freshly ground black pepper

1 tablespoon olive oil

3 tablespoons dry bread crumbs

Put the mint in a small bowl and add the cilantro, garlic, lemon zest, and salt to taste. Add pepper to taste and toss with your fingertips, ensuring that the lemon zest and garlic are evenly dispersed. Set aside.

Put the zucchini, cut side up, on a plate and sprinkle with the ¼ teaspoon salt. Set aside for 15 to 20 minutes.

Pour the olive oil into a sauté pan that is large enough to hold the zucchini in a single layer. (Alternatively, you can use two pans or cook the zucchini in two batches.) Pat the zucchini dry with paper towels and season lightly with pepper. Heat the oil over medium-low heat. Add the zucchini to the pan, cut side down, and cook until they are slightly soft but still holding their shape, as little as 5 minutes, adjusting the heat if necessary to maintain a light golden color. If you are unsure whether they are done, test by tasting a small slice.

Arrange the zucchini on a serving plate, browned side up. Serve while

still warm or let cool to room temperature. Just before serving, toss the bread crumbs with the cilantro-mint gremolata and scatter it over the zucchini.

PAIRINGS

Chicken Breasts Marinated with Lemon, Sage, and Aged Balsamic Vinegar (page 163), Roast Cod with Escargot Butter (page 151)

VARIATION

This seasoned bread crumb–herb mixture can be used as a breading for fish or scallops, or as a surprising alternative to gremolata atop osso buco or short ribs.

A chiffonade of basil would be a good replacement for the cilantro.

WILD RICE WITH MUSHROOMS, CRANBERRIES, AND WALNUT OIL

Helen makes this dish for Thanksgiving every year. Though cranberries are in season roughly from October through December—which is when you are likely to make this—we prefer dried berries for their concentrated sweetness, so focused that even when they are chopped into small bits, you taste it in every bite.

Try to make this dish with naturally grown, hand-harvested wild rice. Despite its name, 80 to 90 percent of wild rice is actually commercially cultivated; therefore it can be laced with pesticides, herbicides, and chemical fertilizer. It also doesn't compare to the nutty, sweet flavor of the real thing. SERVES 6

Coarse salt

1 cup wild rice

½ cup whole rolled oats or barley

½ cup dried cranberries, coarsely chopped

1 tablespoon canola oil or other neutral oil

1½ cups diced portobello or other mushrooms

Freshly ground black pepper to taste

1 cup chopped walnuts

2 shallots, peeled and chopped

1 tablespoon chopped flat-leaf parsley

1 tablespoon walnut oil

Bring two pots of salted water to a gentle boil over high heat. Add the wild rice to one pot, and cook until tender but not mushy, 30 minutes to 1 hour. After 20 minutes, add the oats to the other pot and cook until tender, approximately 15 minutes. Check both occasionally as they cook.

Meanwhile, put the cranberries in a small bowl and cover with warm water. Set aside.

Heat the canola oil in a sauté pan set over medium heat. Add the mushrooms and sauté until they soften and begin to release their liquid, 8 to 10 minutes. Season lightly with salt and pepper, and transfer to a serving bowl.

Add the walnuts, shallots, and parsley to the bowl containing the mushrooms. When the cranberries are soft, drain them and add them to the bowl. When the oats and wild rice are tender, drain them and add them to the bowl.

When all the ingredients have been added, drizzle the mixture with the walnut oil and toss gently. Taste, and adjust the seasoning with salt and pepper if necessary. Serve while still warm or at room temperature.

PAIRINGS

Salmon with Red Wine and Balsamic Vinegar (page 158), Grilled Marinated Pork Chops (page 176)

VARIATIONS

Whole oats have an affinity for nuts. Other grains such as farro will work beautifully as well.

Substitute currants or golden raisins for the cranberries, or extra virgin olive oil and a squeeze of lemon for the walnut oil.

FLAVOR BUILDING

To add extra flavor to the rice and oats, cook them in Chicken Stock (page 31) rather than water.

For a more elegant dish, use chanterelle mushrooms instead of portobello.

SAUTÉED SHELL BEANS WITH PANCETTA

In the summer, farmers' markets are overflowing with shell beans, and I'm always looking for quick and easy recipes that put them to good use. This is one of my favorites, in which the sweet beans are offset by salty pancetta and the bite of red onion and garlic. We usually make it with an assortment of yellow and green beans like the ones featured here, but feel free to substitute your own favorites, such as snow peas, sugar snap peas, and/or Roma beans. SERVES 4 TO 6

3 teaspoons extra virgin olive oil

3 ounces pancetta (about 8 thin slices)

⅓ cup diced red onion

¼ teaspoon finely chopped garlic

½ cup cooked shelled fava beans (see Note)

4 ounces dragon beans or string beans, cooked, cooled, cut into 1-inch pieces (½ cup sliced)

½ cup fresh cooked cranberry beans

½ cup fresh English peas, cooked

Coarse salt

Freshly ground black pepper

Pour 1 teaspoon of the olive oil into a sauté pan and warm it over medium heat. Add the pancetta and sauté until tender-crisp, about 8 minutes. Use tongs or a slotted spoon to remove the pancetta, and set it on a paper towel–lined plate to drain.

Add the onions to the pan and cook for 4 minutes. Add the garlic and cook for 1 minute. Then add the cooked beans and the peas. Add the remaining 2 teaspoons oil, return the pancetta to the pan, toss, and warm through. Season to taste with salt and pepper.

Transfer the contents of the pan to a warmed serving bowl, and serve warm.

Note: Fava beans are purchased in a long, tough pod. To prepare them for cooking, slice the pod open at the seam and remove the beans. Each bean is encased in a thick, white outer shell that must be carefully peeled away before blanching or cooking the beans.

PAIRINGS

Lime and Butter–Braised Fluke (page 152), Sautéed Chicken Breasts with Button Mushrooms and Sage (page 164)

VARIATIONS

Feel free to replace some or all of the beans with your favorites, such as pole or bush beans.

The pancetta can be omitted; start the dish with 2 tablespoons of oil.

FLAVOR BUILDING

Add a last-second, aromatic element by stirring in pea leaves, grated lemon zest, or chopped herbs, such as chervil, basil, mint, parsley, or lemon thyme.

BABY TURNIPS WITH APRICOTS AND PISTACHIOS

This recipe was inspired by the sight of beautiful baby turnips at the farmers' market, with their leafy tops intact. To emphasize their tender flavor, they are paired with apricots and gently poached. The greens are wilted in the same cooking liquid as the turnips. As a final touch, the liquid is reduced, finished with butter, and spooned over the turnips and apricots. SERVES 4

3 bunches baby turnips with their tops (about 20 turnips), cut into ¼-inch-thick rounds, greens washed, dried, and set aside (see Note)

3 tablespoons unsalted butter

2 teaspoons sugar

Coarse salt

Freshly ground white pepper to taste

⅔ cup dried Turkish apricots plumped in 1 cup hot water for 10 minutes, then thickly sliced

3 tablespoons coarsely chopped unsalted pistachios

Put the turnips in a pot and add just enough water to cover by ¼ inch. Add 1 tablespoon of the butter and the sugar, season with salt and pepper, and bring the water to a boil over high heat. Lower the heat so the liquid is just simmering and continue to simmer until the turnips are just tender, 4 to 6 minutes.

Add the apricots and warm them for 1 minute. Add the turnip greens, stir, and let wilt for 1 minute. Season to taste with salt and pepper. Use a slotted spoon to transfer the turnips, apricots, and greens to a large warmed serving bowl and set them aside to keep warm.

Return the pot to the stove and bring the cooking liquid to a boil over high heat. Continue to boil until reduced by one-third to concentrate the flavors, 2 to 3 minutes. (There should be only a few tablespoons of liquid left.) Remove the pot from the heat and whisk or swirl in the remaining 2 tablespoons butter. Taste, and season with salt and pepper.

Spoon the reduction over the turnips, apricots, and greens, sprinkle with the pistachios, and serve.

Note: If you can't find turnips with greens attached, or if the greens don't look good, substitute 2 cups radish greens, watercress, or even arugula.

VARIATION
Medjool dates, pitted and cut into slivers, are a sweet substitute for the apricots.

FLAVOR BUILDING
Sprinkle 1 tablespoon minced chives over the dish along with the pistachios.

PAN-ROASTED MUSHROOMS, CHESTNUTS, AND PEARL ONIONS

In this rustic dish, the autumn trio of chestnuts, cremini mushrooms, and celery root is rounded out with pearl onions and parsley for a perfect accompaniment to poultry and game birds. SERVES 4 TO 6

16 chestnuts (vacuum-packed French chestnuts can be used; skip the roasting step)

4 ounces slab bacon, diced

1 tablespoon olive oil

12 pearl onions, peeled

1 medium celery root, peeled and diced

8 ounces cremini mushrooms, trimmed and thickly sliced

Coarse salt

Freshly ground white pepper to taste

1 teaspoon finely chopped garlic

1 tablespoon unsalted butter

1 tablespoon chopped flat-leaf parsley

Preheat the oven to 425°F.

Score each chestnut with an X on the flat side. Spread them out on a cookie sheet and roast in the oven until fragrant, about 35 minutes, shaking the pan from time to time to keep them from scorching. Remove the pan from the oven and set it aside to let the chestnuts cool. When they are cool enough to handle, remove and discard the shells and coarsely chop the chestnuts. Set aside.

Put the bacon and olive oil in a wide, deep sauté pan set over medium-low heat. Sauté until the bacon is crisp and has rendered enough fat to coat the bottom of the pan, about 6 minutes. Remove the bacon with a slotted spoon and set it on a paper towel–lined plate to drain.

Add the pearl onions and celery root to the pan, raise the heat to medium, and cook, stirring, for 6 minutes. Add the mushrooms, season with salt and pepper, and sauté until the vegetables just begin to soften, 4 to 5 minutes, adding the garlic for the last minute. Return the bacon to the pan and add the chestnuts, butter, and parsley. Toss, taste, and adjust the seasoning with salt and pepper if necessary.

To serve, transfer the contents of the pan to a warmed serving bowl and pass family-style from the center of the table.

PAIRING

Oxtail Braised in Red Wine with Mashed Root Vegetables (page 182)

VARIATION

Black trumpet or chanterelle mushrooms stand in well for the cremini.

FLAVOR BUILDING

Add 1 cup diced apple and/or ½ cup dried cranberries along with the pearl onions to set off the mushrooms with a bit of sweetness.

OVEN-ROASTED MUSHROOMS

It doesn't get any simpler than this: a thoughtful selection of mushrooms tossed with olive oil, garlic, and thyme, then roasted at high heat until they become fragrant and turn a golden brown. A satisfying side dish to almost anything you plan to grill or roast. SERVES 4

8 cups assorted mushrooms (portobello, cremini, oyster, chanterelle), trimmed and cut into large pieces (from about 1½ pounds mushrooms)

1 tablespoon chopped thyme leaves

1 tablespoon chopped garlic

¼ cup extra virgin olive oil

Coarse salt

Freshly ground black pepper

Preheat the oven to 500°F.

In a large bowl, toss the mushrooms with the thyme, garlic, and olive oil. Season with salt and pepper. Spread the mushrooms out in a single layer, in a roasting pan and roast until golden brown and fragrant, about 15 minutes.

To serve, transfer the mushrooms to a warmed serving bowl.

PAIRINGS

Pan-Roasted Squab with Butter-Braised Savoy Cabbage and Green Apples (page 172), Filet Mignon with Madeira Sauce (page 178)

FLAVOR BUILDING

Make roasted garlic along with the mushrooms: Put 20 peeled garlic cloves in a pot, cover them with cold water, bring to a boil over high heat, and boil for 8 to 10 minutes. Drain, and add the cloves to the roasting pan when you put the mushrooms in to roast.

For even more flavor, add toasted pine nuts and rosemary, marjoram, and/or sage sprigs to the mix and drizzle the finished dish with walnut oil.

FENNEL COLESLAW

I came up with this recipe when *New York* magazine asked me to create a dish built around soft-shelled crabs. Technically speaking, this is a coleslaw, but the unconventional presence of basil, fennel seeds, and, of course, the fennel itself makes it fresh and surprising. SERVES 4

1 fennel bulb, tough outer layers removed, tops trimmed, 2 tablespoons chopped fronds reserved

1 carrot, peeled and julienned

1 small Savoy cabbage, cored, outer leaves removed, thinly sliced

½ teaspoon fennel seeds, toasted and ground

½ cup mayonnaise, preferably homemade (page 51)

2 teaspoons freshly squeezed lemon juice

1 tablespoon chopped chives

1 tablespoon basil chiffonade

Coarse salt

Freshly ground white pepper to taste

Using a Japanese mandoline or a very sharp knife, thinly shave the fennel crosswise.

In a bowl, toss together the fennel, carrots, cabbage, and fennel seeds. Add the mayonnaise and toss to nicely coat the slaw. Add the lemon juice, chives, and basil, and toss again. Season to taste with salt and pepper. Transfer to a bowl and serve.

PAIRING

Spicy Grilled Skirt Steak (page 181)

FLAVOR BUILDING

Add 1 tablespoon mustard, mustard seed, or whole-grain mustard to the slaw along with the mayonnaise to punch up the flavor.

POTATO PUREE

The mashed potatoes we serve at the Gotham Bar and Grill have changed slightly over the years. We serve the potato puree with rack of lamb, but it's a perfect accompaniment to a wide variety of meats and fish. Here is the recipe in its current incarnation. SERVES 4

Coarse salt

2½ pounds yellowfin or Red potatoes

²/₃ cup crème fraîche or sour cream

½ cup milk or half-and-half

8 tablespoons (1 stick) cold, unsalted butter, cut into pieces

Freshly ground white pepper

Bring a pot of salted water to a boil over high heat. Add the potatoes and cook until tender, 15 to 20 minutes. Drain well.

Return the potatoes to the pot and cook over medium heat, stirring often, until the excess moisture evaporates and they begin to stick slightly to the bottom of the pan, approximately 3 minutes. Pass the potatoes through a ricer into a large bowl (or use a potato masher), and mash the potatoes with the crème fraîche, milk, and butter. Season with salt and pepper.

The potato puree may be kept warm in the top of a double boiler set over simmering water for up to 2 hours.

PAIRINGS

Roast Cod with a New England Chowder Sauce (page 148), Roast Cod with Escargot Butter (page 151), Lime and Butter–Braised Fluke (page 152), Salmon with Red Wine and Balsamic Vinegar (page 158), Sautéed Chicken Breasts with Button Mushrooms and Sage (page 164)

DESSERTS

APPROPRIATELY ENOUGH, THE DESSERTS THAT FOLLOW
bring this book of simple pleasures full circle, reinforcing many of its themes. In some ways, this chapter isn't as much of a departure for me as the ones that precede it. Because I'm not a formally trained pastry chef, I've always favored relatively simple desserts at home, gravitating toward those that can be prepared in advance and don't call for terribly intricate techniques. I've also always believed that when a meal comprises a certain intensity of flavor, as many of the dishes in this book do, they are best complemented with simple desserts like the ones that follow.

Just as a professional kitchen's pastry department is run by its own chef, several of these recipes have been developed not by me, but by two very talented pastry experts. Many of them were contributed by my wife, Helen Chardack, who worked alongside Deborah Madison at Greens and Alice Waters at Chez Panisse on the West Coast before becoming chef at Jams restaurant in New York City and pastry chef of Gotham Bar and Grill. Others were graciously shared by Gotham's current pastry chef, Deborah Racicot, herself a young veteran of several three-star restaurants.

As is the case throughout the book, international sources have provided much of the inspiration here. Some dishes are presented more or less in their original form, like the Moroccan Oranges with Cinnamon, Honey, and Orange-Flower Water. In other cases, the original dish serves as a stepping-off point, as in Helen's interpretation of British summer pudding or in my adaptation of a dish I learned to make while working in France more than twenty years ago, Cavaillon Melon with Raspberries and Late-Harvest Riesling.

Playfulness is especially appropriate in desserts, so recasting the familiar in a new way proves very impactful, like turning one of the holiday season's true staples into Eggnog Panna Cotta with Caramel Sauce and Brandied Cherries.

Many pastry chefs find that their most popular creations recall childhood favorites, a convention honored here by rethinking a few for an adult audience. We've devised Popsicles made with cilantro and kiwi that will appeal to mature palates; an unexpected take on peanut brittle; and a Strawberry White Chocolate Napoleon that elevates a taken-for-granted bakery treat to the stuff of sophisticated sweetness.

If you're like me, you value desserts that can be made in advance. When entertaining, they allow the cook to remain at the table rather than in the kitchen, and on an everyday basis, they lend desserts longevity, allowing leftovers to be savored the next day or over a few days. We've included several that fit this bill, such as the Walnut Cake with Cranberries and Dates and the Italian Prune Compote with Ginger and Star Anise.

Finally, there are few things more charming in a kitchen than homemade cookies and confections that can be enjoyed at any time. Accordingly, this chapter includes recipes for Coconut Macaroons and Rugalach, two desserts intended for the cookie jar, keeping sweet, simple pleasures within reach at all times.

ORANGES WITH CINNAMON, HONEY, AND ORANGE-FLOWER WATER

At Hotel La Mamounia in Marrakech, extraordinary, formal feasts are served in surroundings that satisfy every traveler's fantasy of Morocco. The multi-course meals, complete with belly dancing and music, often conclude with a surprisingly simple dessert like this one made with orange-flower water, a uniquely Moroccan ingredient that's available from baking and specialty shops. Oranges are available year-round, but for the best flavor, serve this between late December and March, when Honeybell and Minneola oranges are at their peak and bursting with sweet nectar. SERVES 4

3 tablespoons honey

¾ teaspoon orange-flower water

3 or 4 large ripe oranges, preferably Honeybell or Minneola, peeled and cut crosswise into pinwheel slices

About ½ teaspoon ground cinnamon

Leaves from 2 mint sprigs, julienned

In a small bowl, stir the honey with 1½ teaspoons warm water. Stir in the orange-flower water.

Arrange the orange slices on four chilled dessert plates. Drizzle the honey-water mixture over the slices, and sprinkle with the cinnamon. Scatter the mint over the oranges, and serve.

PAIRINGS

Chicken with Olives and Preserved Lemon Sauce (page 169)

VARIATION

Blood oranges or tangelos would also work in this dessert.

FLAVOR BUILDING

Top each serving with chopped toasted pistachios or almonds.

CAVAILLON MELON WITH RASPBERRIES AND LATE-HARVEST RIESLING

While working for the legendary Troisgros brothers in Roanne, France, I was introduced to Cavaillon (or Charentais) melons. With their orange flesh, sublimely sweet flavor, and enticing fragrance they are considered to be among the finest examples of this fruit. Cavaillon melons can be found in specialty markets here in the United States, largely because they are now grown all over the world. Identify them by their smooth, hard rind, a stark contrast to the netted rind of cantaloupes. At Troisgros, these melons were put to use in a dish that inspired this one, in which the flavors of raspberries and melon are united by a late-harvest Riesling or other sweet wine.

Honeydew melon can stand in for the Cavaillon; cut the honeydew into 1-inch dice, toss gently with the raspberries, and serve in chilled martini glasses or on chilled dessert plates. SERVES 4

1 pint raspberries

¾ cup late-harvest Riesling or other sweet wine

2 Cavaillon (Charentais) melons

Mint leaves

Put the raspberries in a bowl and pour the wine over them. Let macerate at room temperature for 20 minutes.

While the raspberries are macerating, halve the melons and use a tablespoon to scoop out and discard the seeds.

To serve, put 1 melon half on each of four chilled soup plates. Divide the berries and wine among the scooped-out melon halves, and garnish with the mint leaves.

PAIRING

Grilled Swordfish with Summer Vegetable Compote (page 161)

VARIATION

Substitute blackberries for the raspberries.

FLAVOR BUILDING

Toss the raspberries with sliced white peaches or nectarines.

SUMMER PLUM PUDDING

Summer pudding is a classic British dessert, originally made by lining a bowl with slices of bread and filling it with a combination of raspberries and red currants. The berry juice seeps into the bread, which soaks up its flavor and color. This summer pudding uses pound cake in place of the bread and, most uniquely, plums in place of the berries. The brilliant color of the plums infuses the entire cake with its brightness. Crumbled gingersnap cookies are added to the filling to help absorb the generous amounts of juice and to add a gently spicy undercurrent. SERVES 6

3 pounds red or black plums

1 cup sugar, plus more for sweetening the crème fraîche

2 tablespoons freshly squeezed lemon juice, plus more if needed

1 tablespoon Grand Marnier, plus more if needed

¾ cup gingersnap cookie crumbs

Canola oil or other neutral-flavored oil

1 small, high-quality, store-bought pound cake (approximately 12 ounces)

Crème fraîche

Prepare the plum filling: Halve each plum, twist the halves apart, and remove the pit. (If the pit refuses to come away, cut the halves in half and pry away a quarter at a time.) Cut the plums into 1-inch pieces. Put the plums in a heavy-bottomed saucepan, and add the 1 cup sugar and 2 tablespoons lemon juice. Set over medium-low heat and stew, covered, stirring occasionally, until the plums are just cooked through and have released their juices, about 15 minutes. Taste, and add more sugar and lemon juice if necessary. Add the 1 tablespoon Grand Marnier and strain the mixture through a fine-mesh sieve set over a bowl. Reserve the liquid (this will become the sauce). Put the strained plums in a bowl and gently stir in the cookie crumbs, leaving out a tablespoon or two for garnish. Set aside.

Prepare the mold: Lightly oil a 6-cup mold or bowl with canola oil. Remove and discard the dark edges of the pound cake. Cut the cake lengthwise into ¼-inch-thick slices. Use the slices to line the bowl, starting with the bottom and cutting the slices to fit the sides. Spoon the plums into the mold, and tap the bowl lightly to settle them. Finish with a layer of cake over the plums. Cover with a plate that fits just inside the rim of the bowl, and place a light weight (such as a can) on top. Refrigerate (weighted) for at least 4 to 5 hours or overnight. Put the sauce in an airtight container and refrigerate it as well.

To serve, unmold the cake onto the center of a large dessert plate. Taste the reserved sauce, and add more Grand Marnier or lemon juice if needed. Transfer some of the sauce to a small bowl and use it to brush the outside of the pudding, creating a beautiful, rich, deep red coat and allowing it to pool around the pudding on the plate.

Serve each slice garnished with lightly sweetened crème fraîche, extra sauce, and a dusting of the reserved cookie crumbs.

PAIRING

Grilled Swordfish with Summer Vegetable Compote (page 161)

VARIATION

Instead of the crème fraîche, garnish with whipped cream sweetened with confectioners' sugar.

FLAVOR BUILDING

Purchase 3 or 4 extra plums, and for a final flourish, top each serving with a fanned-out plum half.

CRANBERRY POACHED PEARS
WITH GINGER AND TEA INFUSION

Usually pears are poached in a mixture of water, white wine, sugar, and citrus juices, or in red wine, sometimes alloyed with port. Then spices and herbs are added to infuse the liquid and fruit with flavor.

This poaching liquid pairs cranberry juice with pears. Not only do pears have a great taste affinity with ginger and cranberry, but they are a perfect visual match with these ingredients as well. (The cranberry juice colors the pears an exquisite pink.) Whichever tea you use will add depth: the Darjeeling will complement the pear with citrus undertones, while the Lapsang Souchong will contribute a touch of smokiness. SERVES 6 TO 8

1½ cups unsweetened cranberry juice (see Note)

¾ cup sugar, plus more if needed

2 quarter-size slices ginger

Juice of 1 orange, plus more if needed

6 Bartlett pears, halved lengthwise and cored

1 Lapsang Souchong or Darjeeling tea bag

1 teaspoon Grand Marnier, optional

6 to 8 mint leaves

Pour the cranberry juice into a medium saucepan. Add 1½ cups water, the ¾ cup sugar, and the ginger, and stir to incorporate. Strain the orange juice into the pan through a fine-mesh sieve. Set the pan over medium-high heat and bring to a boil, stirring until the sugar is completely dissolved.

Add the pear halves to the saucepan, set over medium heat, and simmer gently, submerging the pears occasionally, until barely cooked through, approximately 10 minutes. (Check with the tip of a sharp, thin-bladed knife. Very ripe pears will cook quickly; firm ones take a bit longer.) Using a slotted spoon, transfer the pears to a bowl. Taste the cooking liquid, and adjust with more sugar or orange juice if necessary. If desired, return it to a simmer for a few minutes to thicken slightly.

Pour 2 tablespoons of the hot liquid into a cup and add the tea bag. Steep for 1 minute, then remove the tea bag. Return the steeped liquid to the saucepan, a teaspoon or so at

a time. The tea will have a powerful influence, so taste the liquid in the pan after each addition to ensure a subtle effect. Pour the liquid over the pears, let cool, and refrigerate for at least 1 hour.

To serve, remove the pears from the refrigerator and halve each half lengthwise. Place a few pear pieces in each of six chilled glasses. Spoon some poaching liquid over each serving, and finish with a splash of Grand Marnier, if desired. Add a mint leaf for garnish.

Note: Unsweetened cranberry juice, available at any health food store, is very tart, with a pronounced body and a deep, concentrated ruby color. Cosmopolitan lovers take note: this is the best type of cranberry juice to use in that cocktail.

PAIRINGS

Filet Mignon with Madeira Sauce (page 178), Oxtail Braised in Red Wine with Mashed Root Vegetables (page 182)

ITALIAN PRUNE COMPOTE WITH GINGER AND STAR ANISE

This compote focuses on the fresh Italian prune plums, which are available in late summer. They are recognizable by their elongated shape, deep purple skin, and yellow flesh. Infused with the flavor of star anise, this compote can be eaten on its own, served alongside a moist cake such as a lemon pound cake, or served over vanilla ice cream. SERVES 4 TO 6

3 tablespoons sugar

1 tablespoon unsalted butter

1 tablespoon honey

½ vanilla bean, split, seeds scraped

3 whole star anise

1 teaspoon freshly squeezed lemon juice

2 pounds medium-ripe Italian prune plums or Empress plums, halved and pitted

¼ teaspoon fine salt

3 tablespoons Muscat de Beaumes-de-Venise or other sweet white wine

¼ teaspoon grated ginger

Pour the sugar into a 12-inch sauté pan and heat it over medium heat until it has melted, 6 minutes. Add the butter, honey, vanilla, star anise, and lemon juice.

Sprinkle the cut side of the plums with the salt and set them in the pan, cut side down. Raise the heat and cook until lightly caramelized and beginning to soften, 4 to 6 minutes. Add the wine and ginger, and turn the plums over. Lower the heat and cook until they are soft and brightly fuchsia-tinted, about 5 more minutes. Remove the pan from the heat and allow the prunes to cool in their syrup.

FLAVOR BUILDING

Chopped pistachios, toasted almonds, or crushed amaretto cookies would be a nice finishing touch.

POPSICLES

Because most people regard Popsicles as a kids-only proposition, they're a surprising treat for adults. These popsicles veer away from the simple, artificially created flavor of the mass-produced (cherry, grape, orange) toward more natural and sophisticated fresh juices and combinations.

These depend on a foundation of fresh juice, pureed fruit, and simple syrup. By all means use them as a blueprint to create Popsicles of your own invention.

Note that each recipe requires 4-ounce Popsicle molds. MAKES 8 TO 10 POPSICLES

WATERMELON

2 cups pureed seedless watermelon flesh (from about 2 pounds watermelon weighed with the rind)

2 pints raspberries (approximately 2 cups)

3 tablespoons freshly squeezed lime juice

½ cup simple syrup (see Note)

Pinch of fine salt

Put the watermelon, raspberries, lime juice, syrup, and salt in a blender and puree until smooth. Pass the mixture through a fine-mesh sieve into a bowl, pressing down on the solids to extract as much liquid as possible. Pour the strained liquid into Popsicle molds and freeze for 1 hour. Center a Popsicle stick in each well, and freeze overnight.

KIWI-TANGERINE

1 cup freshly squeezed tangerine juice (from about 3 tangerines)

1½ cups pureed kiwi flesh (from about 4 kiwis)

1½ cups simple syrup (see Note)

Pinch of fine salt

Put the tangerine juice and kiwi puree in a blender and blend. Strain the mixture through a fine-mesh sieve set over a bowl, pressing down to extract as much liquid as possible. Stir in ½ cup water, the syrup, and the salt. Divide the mixture among Popsicle molds and freeze for 1 hour. Center a Popsicle stick in each well, and freeze overnight.

Note: To make ½ cup simple syrup, pour ½ cup water into a small pot. Stir in ½ cup sugar and set the pot over high heat. Bring the mixture to a boil and continue to boil until the sugar has dissolved. Remove the pot from the heat and let cool completely. To make 1½ cups syrup, use 1 cup water and 1 cup sugar.

LIME-CILANTRO

½ cup milk

1 cup sugar

½ cup cilantro leaves

½ cup freshly squeezed lime juice

Pinch of fine salt

Fill a large bowl halfway with ice cubes.

Put the milk, ½ cup water, the sugar, and the the cilantro in a saucepan, and stir together. Bring to a boil over high heat. Remove the pan from the heat and set aside to let the liquid steep for 10 minutes. Then cool it as quickly as possible by setting it on the ice cubes and stirring the liquid with a wooden spoon.

Pour the cooled mixture into a blender, add the lime juice and salt, and blend until smooth. Pour the mixture through a fine-mesh sieve set over a bowl, pressing down on the solids to extract as much liquid as possible. Divide the liquid among the Popsicle molds and freeze for 1 hour. Center a Popsicle stick in each well, and freeze overnight.

APPLE FRANGIPANE WITH
DRIED CHERRIES, RAISINS, AND RUM

In place of a pastry shell, this recipe uses a fluted pie dish to hold a quick mix of stewed apples, cherries, raisins, and rum. An almond cream is fashioned from butter, almonds, egg, and amaretti cookies (the fragrant Italian macaroon made with bitter almonds), then spooned over the apples before the dish is baked. The custard sets up and turns golden brown and chewy, not unlike the filling of an almond croissant, a similarity bolstered by topping the dessert with slivered almonds.

This recipe is easily doubled or tripled. SERVES 6 TO 8

⅓ cup mixed dried sour cherries and golden raisins

4 tablespoons dark rum

4 large apples, peeled, quartered, cored, and cut into ½-inch slices

4 tablespoons soft, unsalted butter, at room temperature

⅔ cup granulated sugar

1 tablespoon apple cider

½ cup crushed Italian amaretti cookies

½ cup ground almonds

½ cup confectioners' sugar, plus more for dusting

1 tablespoon cornstarch

1 large egg, beaten

⅓ cup sliced almonds

Vanilla ice cream

Preheat the oven to 375°F.

Put the dried fruit and 2 tablespoons of the rum in a small saucepan. Bring to a boil, then remove the pan from the heat and set aside.

Put the apples and 1 tablespoon of the butter in a sauté pan set over low heat. Stew for 2 minutes, then gently stir in the granulated sugar and cider and continue cooking until the apples are almost cooked through, approximately 3 more minutes. Transfer the apples to a large bowl to cool them as quickly as possible. Add the raisins, cherries, and remaining 2 tablespoons rum to the hot apples, stir, and set aside to cool.

In a small bowl, stir together the remaining 3 tablespoons of the butter, the crushed cookies, ground almonds, ½ cup confectioners' sugar, cornstarch, and egg.

Transfer the cooled apples to a fluted pie dish that can be brought to the table, lightly packing them. Level the surface, and spread the almond mixture over the top.

Scatter the sliced almonds on top, and bake until golden brown, 30 to 40 minutes.

Remove the dish from the oven and let cool. Dust the dessert with confectioners' sugar before serving. Serve it with vanilla ice cream.

PAIRINGS

Roast Cod with a New England Chowder Sauce (page 148), Sautéed Chicken Breasts with Button Mushrooms and Sage (page 164), Braised Pork with Fennel and Red Bliss Potatoes (page 174)

WALNUT CAKE WITH CRANBERRIES AND DATES

The Italian *panforte* is a once-common Christmas pastry, also known as Siena cake because it is a specialty of that town. It's a dense, chewy confection made with honey, candied fruits, hazelnuts, almonds, cocoa, spices, and just enough flour to bind these ingredients together. When baked, it becomes very chewy, resembling a confection more than a cake.

While this cake bears little visual or textural relation to a *panforte,* it does use many of the same flavors. It can easily be made ahead and served the following day(s)—just wrap it well and set it aside on the counter. Serve it with Vin Santo, the sweet Italian dessert wine, or espresso.

P.S. A small slice is a delightful breakfast indulgence. SERVES 8

1 generous tablespoon good-quality, chunky orange marmalade

8 tablespoons (1 stick) unsalted butter, at room temperature

½ cup granulated sugar

2 eggs, at room temperature

1 cup ground walnuts (see Notes)

1 cup plain cookie crumbs (see Notes), from sugar cookies or vanilla wafers

½ cup coarsely chopped dried cranberries

½ cup chopped dates (see Notes)

2 tablespoons all-purpose flour

1 teaspoon baking powder

Confectioners' sugar

Preheat the oven to 375°F.

Cut a sheet of parchment paper to fit the bottom of a 9-inch cake pan. Set it in the pan, and butter and flour the sides and the lined bottom of the pan.

Put the marmalade in a small strainer over a bowl. Allow some of the jelly to pass through, leaving the peel. It does not need to be totally strained. Coarsely chop the peel. Discard the strained jelly.

Cream the butter and sugar together in a mixing bowl with a rubber spatula. (This is easily done by hand if the butter is soft. Otherwise, use a standing mixer.) Whisk in the eggs, one at a time. Then fold in the walnuts and cookie crumbs. Stir in the chopped cranberries, dates, and orange peel.

Whisk together the flour and baking powder in a separate small bowl. Dust this over the batter mixture and stir to combine. Transfer the batter to the prepared cake pan, and bake until the top is a beautiful walnut brown, about 30 minutes. Remove the pan from the oven and let cool.

Unmold the cake onto a flat surface. Gently turn it face up, and dust it lightly with confectioners' sugar. Transfer it to a large flat dessert plate, slice, and serve.

Notes: Grind the walnuts in a food processor fitted with the metal blade, taking care to not over-process them and turn them to butter. Crush the cookies with a rolling pin or use a hand-held rotary grater, which will also work just fine. Sprinkle a tablespoon or so of sugar over the dates before chopping them, to keep the pieces from sticking together.

CHOCOLATE-GRAND MARNIER CAKE

Rich, semisweet chocolate and the orange intensity of Grand Marnier were made for each other, a fact celebrated here with a dessert featuring a layer of chocolate cake and a layer of Grand Marnier mousse. This is elegant but not complicated—the cake layer and the kumquat garnish can be prepared ahead of time.

The technique for making the flavored cream is worth noting for other applications: by incorporating the liqueur as you whip the cream, the mixture becomes stabilized, unifying the two ingredients. MAKES ONE 9-INCH CAKE

3½ cups heavy cream

¼ cup Grand Marnier

21 ounces Valrhona 66% chocolate (semisweet), coarsely chopped

2 eggs, at room temperature

7 egg yolks, at room temperature

½ cup sugar

1 tablespoon light corn syrup

Chocolate Sponge Cake (recipe follows)

Grated zest of 1 orange

Poached Kumquats (recipe follows)

Pour 2 cups of the cream and the Grand Marnier into the bowl of a standing mixer fitted with the whip attachment. Whip until soft peaks form. Transfer the whipped cream to a clean bowl and set aside. Wipe out the mixing bowl and clean the whip.

Fill a saucepan halfway with water, and bring to a simmer. Put 13 ounces of the chocolate in a stainless steel bowl, and set the bowl over the simmering water. Stir the chocolate just until it melts, taking care to not let it become excessively hot. Set aside.

Put the eggs and yolks in the clean mixing bowl, return the bowl to the mixer, and whip on high speed until pale yellow and ribbony, 4 minutes. Meanwhile, pour the sugar and corn syrup into a saucepan and bring to 240°F (soft ball stage) over high heat.

Lower the speed on the mixer and slowly pour the hot sugar syrup down the side of the bowl so it is incorporated slowly and doesn't cook the eggs. Continue to whip until the mixture cools to room temperature.

Fold one-third of the egg mixture into the melted chocolate. Continue, adding the eggs in two more batches, folding until incorporated. Then fold 2 cups of the whipped cream into the chocolate mixture until incorporated, and set the mousse aside.

Using a circle of cardboard with a 9-inch diameter as your guide, trim the cake to form a 9-inch round. Place the cardboard circle in the bottom of a 9-inch springform pan, and place the cake round on top of the cardboard. Pour the mousse evenly over the cake layer until it is ¼ inch from the top of the pan. Put the pan in the freezer for at least 4 hours, or overnight.

Pour the remaining 1½ cups cream into a small saucepan. Add the orange zest and bring to a simmer over low heat. Remove the pan from the heat and let steep for 5 minutes. Then strain the mixture, discarding the solids, and set it aside.

When you are ready to finish the cake, make the chocolate glaze: Fill a saucepan halfway with water and bring it to a simmer. Put the

CHOCOLATE SPONGE CAKE

The sponge cake can be made the day before you plan to make this dessert. Wrap well in plastic wrap and refrigerate for up to three days or freeze for up to one week.

remaining 8 ounces chocolate in a stainless steel bowl. Set the bowl over the simmering water and stir the chocolate just until it melts, taking care to not let it become excessively hot. Set it aside.

Return the orange-flavored cream to a small saucepan and reheat it over low heat. Pour it over the melted chocolate and whisk until smooth.

Remove the cake from the freezer and pour the chocolate glaze over the top, using a baking spatula to scrape off the excess and shape a smooth surface. Return the cake to the freezer for 15 minutes to set the glaze.

Wet a towel under hot tap water and squeeze until just damp. Wrap the towel around the sides of the springform pan to keep the cake from sticking. Unclasp the sides of the pan, and unmold. Transfer the cake with its cardboard base onto a serving platter and let the cake defrost for 1 hour before serving. Cut into slices, and garnish each slice with 2 tablespoons of the poached kumquats.

5 eggs, separated, at room temperature

¾ cup sugar

½ cup unsweetened cocoa powder

Preheat the oven to 350°F.

Put the egg yolks and ¼ cup of the sugar in the bowl of a standing mixer fitted with the whip attachment. Whip until thick and ribbony, approximately 10 minutes. Transfer the mixture to a clean bowl and set aside. Wipe out the mixing bowl and clean the whip.

Put the whites in the mixing bowl, return the bowl to the mixer, and whip on medium speed until foamy. Slowly add the remaining ½ cup sugar, continuing to whip until the whites are stiff and shiny.

Sift one-third of the cocoa powder into the egg yolks, folding slowly. Then fold in one-third of the egg whites. Continue, alternating additions of sifted cocoa powder and egg whites, until all of the ingredients are incorporated.

Spray a 13 by 9-inch baking dish with nonstick cooking spray, and line the bottom with parchment paper. Pour the batter into the dish, spreading it out evenly.

Bake the cake for 10 minutes. Then rotate the dish and continue to bake for 5 more minutes, or until the cake springs back when pressed with a finger.

Invert the cake onto a cooling rack, unmold it, and let it cool completely.

POACHED KUMQUATS

These are delicious on their own, topped with whipped cream.

1 pint kumquats

1½ cups simple syrup (see Note, page 227)

Using a paring knife, slice the kumquats into ⅛-inch-thick rounds, removing the seeds as you work.

Put the simple syrup in a small saucepan and bring to a simmer over low heat. Add the kumquats and remove from the heat. Let the kumquats sit in the hot syrup until completely cooled. They should still be a bit firm. These kumquats can be covered and refrigerated for up to 1 week.

PINEAPPLE-CARROT CAKE

A riff on carrot cake, with pineapple and coconut added for their distinct sweetness, this pleasingly moist cake is completed by the lime-infused pineapple that's served alongside. It's especially good with a scoop of coconut sorbet.

Note that you will need a triangle-shaped metal terrine mold (3½ inches high, 19 inches long, and 3½ inches wide at the base), or a rectangular mold (2½ inches high, 2½ inches wide, and 19 inches long).

SERVES 8 TO 10

½ cup plus 2 tablespoons sugar

¼ cup plus 2 tablespoons canola oil

1 egg

½ teaspoon fine salt

½ teaspoon ground cinnamon

½ teaspoon baking powder

½ cup all-purpose flour

¼ cup shredded fresh golden pineapple, drained, plus 2 cups diced fresh pineapple

½ cup finely shredded carrots

¼ cup unsweetened flaked coconut

Grated zest and juice of 1 lime

Store-bought coconut sorbet, optional

Preheat the oven to 350°F.

Put the ½ cup sugar and the canola oil in the bowl of a standing mixer fitted with the paddle attachment, and paddle until creamed together, approximately 2 minutes. Add the egg and mix well.

Sift the salt, cinnamon, baking powder, and flour together in a bowl. Add this to the egg mixture and mix well, scraping down the sides of the bowl with a rubber spatula. Add the shredded pineapple, carrots; and coconut, and mix well.

Spray the mold (see headnote) with nonstick cooking spray, and pour in the batter; it should reach two-thirds of the way up its sides. Bake for 15 minutes. Then rotate the pan and bake until the cake is browned on top or until a paring knife inserted in the center comes out clean, 7 to 10 minutes. Remove the cake from the oven and set it aside to cool.

Meanwhile, mix together the diced pineapple, lime zest and juice, and remaining 2 tablespoons sugar.

When the cake has cooled completely, unmold the cake onto a cutting board, and cut it into thick slices. Divide the slices among individual plates, and serve with some of the diced pineapple alongside. Add a topping of coconut sorbet, if desired.

PAIRING

Spicy Grilled Skirt Steak (page 181)

LIME MERINGUE TARTS

Based on lemon meringue pie, these individual tartlets are instead made with lime, with an almond crust providing a firm, chewy base. With the exception of the meringue, these can be prepared ahead of time, making them ideal for entertaining. MAKES 8 TARTS

ALMOND DOUGH

1½ cups all-purpose flour

2 tablespoons confectioners' sugar

½ teaspoon fine salt

8 tablespoons (1 stick) cold unsalted butter, cut into cubes

¼ cup solid vegetable shortening

½ cup finely chopped, toasted slivered almonds

3 to 4 tablespoons ice water

LIME CURD

½ cup freshly squeezed lime juice (from 8 to 10 limes), plus grated zest of 1 lime

½ cup granulated sugar

4 eggs

4 egg yolks

8 tablespoons (1 stick) unsalted butter, at room temperature, cut into 8 pieces

MERINGUE

3 egg whites, at room temperature

½ cup granulated sugar

½ teaspoon cream of tartar

Prepare the almond crust: Put the flour, confectioners' sugar, salt, butter, shortening, and almonds in the bowl of a standing mixer fitted with the paddle attachment. Paddle until the mixture resembles coarse cornmeal, 2 to 3 minutes. Add the ice water and paddle just enough to bring the dough together and moisten it.

Remove the dough and pat it out to form a disk approximately 6 inches in diameter. Wrap it in plastic wrap and chill it in the refrigerator for 1 hour.

Remove the dough from the refrigerator and roll it out on a lightly floured surface to a thickness of ⅛ inch. Use a 5-inch cookie cutter to cut out eight disks. Press each disk into a 3-inch tart ring, covering the bottom and sides. Chill in the refrigerator for 1 hour.

Preheat the oven to 325°F.

Line each tart crust with parchment paper and weight it down with pie weights or dried beans. Arrange the tarts on 1 or 2 cookie sheets and bake for 15 minutes. Then remove the tarts from the oven and remove the parchment paper. Return the tarts to the oven and continue baking until golden brown, approximately 5 minutes. Remove the tarts from the oven and set them aside to cool.

The tart crusts can be stored in airtight plastic containers, in a single layer, for up to 24 hours.

Prepare the lime curd: Put the lime juice, zest, sugar, eggs, and yolks in a stainless steel bowl and whisk well.

Fill a saucepan halfway with water, and bring the water to a boil over high heat, then lower the heat so the water is simmering. Set the bowl over the pot and whisk the lime mixture occasionally until it thickens, approximately 10 minutes. Then whisk in the butter, 1 piece at a time.

Transfer the mixture to a blender or food processor, and blend until very smooth.

The mixture can be made, cooled, covered, and refrigerated for up to 1 week.

Divide the mixture among the tart shells, and chill in the refrigerator for 1 to 2 hours or until set.

Prepare the meringue and finish the tarts: In the bowl of a standing mixer fitted with the whip attachment, whip the egg whites until frothy. Slowly add the sugar, then the cream of tartar, continuing to whip until well incorporated. Then, with the whip on medium speed, whip until the whites are stiff and shiny. Do not overwhip or they will become grainy.

Transfer the meringue into a pastry bag fitted with a star tip, and pipe it around the edge of each tart. Or transfer it into a large freezer bag, seal tightly, and snip off one corner.

Preheat the broiler.

Put the tarts under the broiler for 1 minute to turn the meringue golden. (You could also brown them with a small kitchen torch.) Serve.

Note: The tarts can be browned, cooled, and refrigerated, uncovered, for up to 4 hours.

PAIRING

Pan-Roasted Squab with Butter-Braised Savoy Cabbage and Green Apples (page 172)

STRAWBERRY WHITE CHOCOLATE NAPOLEON

Strawberry shortcake was the inspiration for this dessert, a simplified version of one we serve in the summertime at Gotham Bar and Grill. Instead of a bowl of strawberries and whipped cream topped with a biscuit, it takes the form of a napoleon and uses white chocolate mousse in place of the whipped cream. Making puff pastry from scratch is enormously time consuming, so this recipe calls on store-bought phyllo dough that's brushed with butter and sugar, stacked, and lightly caramelized. SERVES 8

1 box (1 pound) phyllo sheets, defrosted overnight in the refrigerator

2 cups (4 sticks) unsalted butter, diced and clarified (see Note)

1 box (1 pound) confectioners' sugar, plus more for dusting the napoleons

1 pound 6 ounces white chocolate (ideally Valrhona)

About 2 cups heavy cream

¾ tablespoon powdered gelatin

1¼ cups milk

¼ cup granulated sugar

1 tablespoon vanilla extract

5 egg yolks

1½ cups crème fraîche

3 pints strawberries, sliced

Prepare the phyllo: Preheat the oven to 350°F.

Lay the stack of phyllo sheets off to the side of your work surface and cover it with a slightly damp cloth to prevent drying and cracking. As you remove each sheet of phyllo dough, be sure to replace the towel.

Set 1 sheet of dough on your work surface and use a pastry brush to lightly coat it with clarified butter. With a sifter, gently and evenly dust the surface with confectioners' sugar. Place another phyllo sheet on top of the dusted one. Repeat the layers two more times, using four layers of phyllo in all and finishing the top layer with butter but no sugar. Set the stack aside. Repeat this process three more times, making four sets in all. Put two pieces of parchment paper between them, and stack the phyllo sets on top of one another.

Use an 8-inch metal saucepan lid or cardboard round to guide you in cutting a circle out of the phyllo stack with a knife. Discard the excess dough from outside the circle.

Using the same 8-inch circle as a guide, draw a circle on parchment paper and cut it out. Fold the circle in half, then fold it in half twice more so that, when unfolded, you can see eight perfect triangle creases on the paper.

Place the parchment circle on top of the phyllo stack. Score the edges of the phyllo where the triangle divisions occur, remove the paper, and cut the stack of phyllo into eight perfect triangles. Separate the triangle stacks and arrange them on a parchment-paper-lined cookie sheet. Place another cookie sheet on top to sandwich the phyllo. Put the sheets in the oven and bake, rotating and checking occasionally, until the phyllo is golden brown, 5 to 10 minutes. Remove from the oven and set aside while you make the mousse.

Make the mousse: Chop the chocolate and put it in a glass bowl. Microwave it for 1 minute at high power, then take it out and stir it. If it has not melted completely, return the bowl to the microwave for 20-second intervals until melted. (If you don't have a microwave, put the chopped chocolate in a small metal bowl over a pot of simmering water and let it melt, but be sure to not let it get too hot; white chocolate breaks easily.) Set aside to cool.

Pour ¾ cup of the cream into the bowl of a standing mixer fitted with the whisk attachment, to make 2 cups of whipped cream with medium peaks. Set aside.

Put 2 tablespoons cold water in a small bowl, add the gelatin, and let it bloom, 3 minutes.

Pour the milk into a small saucepan, and add the remaining 1¼ cups cream, the sugar, and the vanilla. Bring to a simmer over medium-low heat. Meanwhile, put the egg yolks in a bowl. When the milk mixture simmers, slowly and gently whisk it into the yolks, taking care to not let them cook. Pour the mixture back into the saucepan. Return the pan to low heat and cook until the custard coats the back of a wooden spoon, 2 to 3 minutes. Working quickly, spoon 1¼ cups of the custard into the bowl containing the gelatin. Whisk, then strain through a fine-mesh sieve into the bowl containing the melted chocolate. Whisk well. Gently fold in the whipped cream. Pour the mousse mixture into a baking pan and chill in the

refrigerator until firm, approximately 5 hours.

Transfer the mousse to the bowl of a standing mixer fitted with the whip attachment. Pour in the crème fraîche, and whip until well incorporated and stiff. Transfer the whipped mousse to a pastry bag fitted with a star tip, or to a large freezer bag, seal tightly, and snip off one corner.

Arrange eight phyllo triangles on a large serving platter, and pipe a layer of mousse over each one. Add a layer of strawberries. Pipe some more mousse on top, and balance a layer of phyllo on the mousse. Repeat the layers of mousse, berries, mousse, and phyllo. Finish the top layer with a sifting of confectioners' sugar, and garnish with the remaining strawberries. Serve.

Note: To clarify butter, put the diced butter in a small saucepan over low heat and let it melt completely. As it simmers, the fat will rise to the top and turn to a white foam. Skim off the foam. Continue to simmer until the butter becomes clear, approximately 10 minutes, keeping an eye on it to ensure it doesn't brown. Pour the clarified butter into a metal or heatproof glass container, and let cool. The clarified butter can be covered and refrigerated for up to 1 week.

EGGNOG PANNA COTTA WITH CARAMEL SAUCE AND BRANDIED CHERRIES

This is a new way to enjoy one of the traditional flavors of the holiday season: eggnog, the ridiculously rich drink made with cream, eggs, sugar, and spiked with a liquor, usually spiced rum. Here, eggnog becomes the basis for a panna cotta, the Italian dessert whose name means "cooked cream." The requisite liquor is represented with a caramel sauce adorned with brandied cherries, a flourish that makes this elegant and enjoyable enough for even the most formal holiday affair. SERVES 6

2 envelopes (2¼ teaspoons each) powdered gelatin

1 quart of your favorite store-bought eggnog

Caramel Sauce and Brandied Cherries (recipe follows)

6 to 8 mint sprigs

Pour 2 tablespoons water into a bowl. Sprinkle the gelatin over it and let it soften and bloom, 3 minutes. Fill a large, wide bowl halfway with ice water and set aside.

Pour the eggnog into a saucepan set over medium heat and bring it to a simmer. Immediately remove the pan from the heat and whisk in the gelatin mixture. Set the bottom of the pan in the ice water and stir until slightly cooled. Divide the eggnog mixture among six 6-ounce ramekins, cover with plastic wrap, and refrigerate for at least 3 hours.

To serve, dip each ramekin in warm water for 2 seconds to loosen the panna cotta from its mold. Invert the ramekin over the center of a dessert plate. (It may be necessary to shake gently to release the custards.) Spoon some sauce and cherries over and around each panna cotta, and garnish with mint sprigs.

CARAMEL SAUCE AND
BRANDIED CHERRIES

⅔ cup dried sour cherries

⅔ cup plus 2 tablespoons sugar

½ cup apple juice

½ cup brandy or Cognac

1 teaspoon freshly squeezed
lemon juice

Put the dried cherries and 2
tablespoons sugar in a small
saucepan. Add the apple juice and
brandy, and set over medium heat.
Bring the liquid to a simmer and
cook gently until the cherries are
softened, about 15 minutes.
Remove the pan from the heat,
cover, and set aside.

Put the remaining ⅔ cup sugar and
3 tablespoons water in a small,
heavy-bottomed saucepan. Set over
medium-high heat and bring the
water to a boil, stirring to dissolve
the sugar. While the sugar is
cooking, drain the cherries and
measure the liquid. There should
be ½ cup. If there is less, add more
brandy or apple juice; if there is
more, discard the excess.

Dip a small brush in water and
brush down any sugar crystals that
have formed on the sides of the
saucepan. Keep stirring the sugar
syrup until the mixture caramelizes
to a rich golden brown,
approximately 4 minutes.

When the sugar reaches the
desired color, remove the pan from
the heat and carefully add the
cherry liquid to stop the cooking.
(Expect it to sputter and boil a
bit.) Return the pan to medium-
low heat and stir. Add the cherries
and lemon juice.

This sauce will thicken as it cools
to room temperature. Its
consistency can be adjusted by
adding a splash of brandy or apple
juice. Refrigerate if not using in
the next several hours. It will keep
for up to 1 week.

PAIRINGS

Pan-Roasted Squab with Butter-
Braised Savoy Cabbage and Green
Apples (page 172), Oxtail Braised in
Red Wine with Mashed Root
Vegetables (page 182)

VARIATION

Serve the Caramel Sauce and
Brandied Cherries over ice cream;
it's perhaps best over simple vanilla.

YOGURT MOUSSE WITH RED BERRY COMPOTE

This dessert, a smart-looking, modern adaptation of a charlotte russe, is made with a brilliant assortment of mixed fresh berries. It features a lime-flavored variation of the traditional Bavarian cream, with cake on the inside rather than lady fingers on the outside. The raspberry granité is an optional accompaniment, but it is easy to make it in advance— or you can replace it with store-bought raspberry sorbet.

You will need twelve stainless steel ring molds, 2 inches in diameter and 2 inches high. SERVES 10 TO 12

BUTTERMILK CAKE

12 tablespoons (1½ sticks) unsalted butter, at room temperature

1½ cups sugar

3 eggs, at room temperature

1 teaspoon vanilla extract

1¾ cups cake flour

1½ teaspoons baking powder

½ teaspoon baking soda

¼ teaspoon fine salt

1 cup buttermilk

YOGURT MOUSSE

1 cup plus 2 tablespoons heavy cream

5 egg yolks, at room temperature

1 cup plus 1 tablespoon sugar

About ¼ cup freshly squeezed lime juice (from about 3 limes)

1¾ tablespoons powdered gelatin

2¼ cups plain yogurt

¼ cup sour cream

Grated zest of 1 lime

Red Berry Compote (recipe follows)

Raspberry Granité (recipe follows), optional

Mint leaves, optional

Prepare the cake: Preheat the oven to 325°F.

Put the butter and sugar in the bowl of a standing mixer fitted with the paddle attachment and cream them together until the mixture is fluffy, approximately 3 minutes. Add the eggs and vanilla, and mix well.

In another bowl, sift together the flour, baking powder, baking soda, and salt. Add alternating quantities of the flour mixture and the buttermilk to the egg mixture, and continue to mix until all is combined.

Line the bottoms of two 8-inch cake pans with parchment, or spray them with nonstick cooking spray and dust them lightly with flour. Divide the batter between the pans, and bake for 20 minutes. The cake is done when it springs back when pressed with a finger, or when a toothpick inserted in the center comes out clean. If the cake(s) need more time, rotate them and continue baking until your tester comes out clean. Remove the cakes from the oven and set them aside to cool completely, then unmold.

The cakes can be made up to 1 day ahead of time. Wrap well in plastic wrap and refrigerate them to firm them up and facilitate slicing.

Make the yogurt mousse: Put the heavy cream in the bowl of a standing mixer fitted with the whip attachment, and whip until stiff. Transfer the whipped cream to another bowl, and set aside in the refrigerator. Wipe out the mixer bowl and clean the whip.

Put the egg yolks in the clean mixer bowl and whip until they are thick and ribbony, approximately 5 minutes.

While the yolks are whipping, put the sugar and ½ cup water in a small saucepan and bring to a boil over medium heat, cooking until the temperature reaches 240°F (soft ball stage). While the sugar is cooking, put the lime juice in a small pot and add the gelatin. Put the yogurt, sour cream, and lime zest in a bowl and whisk well.

When the sugar syrup reaches the desired temperature, slowly pour it down the side of the bowl containing the yolks without touching the whisk, so it doesn't splatter. Continue to whip the yolks until they are just warm.

Heat the lime juice mixture briefly over very low heat, just until the gelatin is dissolved. Then whisk it into the yolks.

Put the yolks in a large bowl, and in three stages, fold in the yogurt mixture. Once it is combined, add the whipped cream. Chill the mousse in the refrigerator until it begins to thicken, approximately 30 minutes.

Assemble the dessert: Slice the cakes horizontally into ¼-inch-thick rounds. Using the ring molds (see headnote), cut out 12 circles and set them aside. Then use a round cookie cutter, approximately 1½ inches in diameter, to cut out 24 circles slightly smaller in diameter than the 12 you have already made. (The larger rings will be used as the base of each individual dessert; the smaller rings will be used for the second and third layers.)

Put the ring molds on a parchment paper–lined cookie sheet. Put 1 large cut-out cake circle in the bottom of each ring. Fill the ring with mousse to a height of about ½ inch. (The mousse may still be a bit loose.) Put the molds in the freezer for 15 minutes to set the mousse.

Remove the sheet from the freezer, and top each portion of mousse with a small cake circle. Cover with 2 tablespoons of mousse, and freeze again for 15 minutes. Repeat once more, making sure that the mousse covers the cake completely. Freeze for 2 hours.

To unmold, rub each ring with your hands to warm the ring and loosen the cake and push the mousse cake out from the bottom. Let the cakes defrost in the refrigerator for 30 minutes.

To serve, put a portion of cake on a plate and spoon 2 to 3 tablespoons of the fruit compote around the base. Sprinkle a few currants over the other berries, and garnish the top with a nice strand of currants. Ganish with a mint leaf and a scoop of raspberry granité, if desired.

RED BERRY COMPOTE

MAKES 6 CUPS, ENOUGH TO SERVE 10 TO 12 AS AN ACCOMPANIMENT

1 pint strawberries, quartered

1 pint raspberries

1 pint blueberries, halved

¼ cup honey

Juice of 1 lime

Pinch of fine salt

1 pint red currants

Put the strawberries, raspberries, and blueberries in a bowl. Drizzle with the honey and lime juice, sprinkle with the salt, and toss lightly. Let macerate for 15 to 20 minutes at room temperature. Hold the currants aside to use as a garnish.

RASPBERRY GRANITÉ

SERVES 12

6 pints raspberries

1 tablespoon grated orange zest, plus the juice of 1 orange

3 whole star anise

2 cups sugar

Pinch of fine salt

Fill a large bowl halfway with ice water.

Put the raspberries in a blender and puree until smooth. Pass the puree through a fine-mesh sieve into a medium saucepan. Add all the other ingredients plus 5 cups of water. Stir and bring to a simmer over medium heat. Remove from the heat and let steep for 10 minutes. Then pass the mixture through a fine-mesh sieve into a bowl. Cool completely by placing the bowl in the bowl of ice water.

Once the mixture is cool, pour it into a baking pan, wrap with plastic wrap, and freeze overnight. The next day, use a fork to scrape the granité until it is nice and fluffy. Divide it among individual serving cups and serve, or use as a garnish with another dessert.

CHOCOLATE-HAZELNUT TIRAMISÙ

Do you know anyone who doesn't love Nutella, the Italian chocolate-hazelnut spread? I don't. Helen likes it so much that she made it the basis for this tiramisù. This recipe is otherwise fairly traditional—ladyfingers, mascarpone, espresso—but the addition of Nutella makes it an even more decadent indulgence. SERVES 12

2 cups heavy cream

8 egg yolks

⅓ cup (lightly packed) light brown sugar

2 tablespoons vanilla extract

1 cup mascarpone

¾ cup Nutella

1½ cups brewed espresso or strong coffee

¼ cup Kahlúa, optional

36 Italian lady fingers

Unsweetened cocoa powder

Pour the cream into the bowl of a standing mixer fitted with the whip attachment, and whip until soft peaks form. Set aside in the refrigerator.

Fill a saucepan halfway with water and bring it to a simmer. Prepare a large bowl of ice water.

Make the zabaglione: In a large stainless steel mixing bowl, whisk together the egg yolks, brown sugar, vanilla, and 3 tablespoons water. Set this over the pot of simmering water, and whisk briskly until the egg mixture triples in volume and holds a soft peak, approximately 8 minutes. Remove the bowl from the simmering water and set it in the bowl of ice water. Whisk until the zabaglione is cool.

Put the mascarpone in a medium bowl. Fold in half of the zabaglione, followed by one-third of the whipped cream. Set aside. Put the Nutella in another bowl, and fold in the remaining half of the zabaglione, followed by the remaining two-thirds of the whipped cream.

Pour the espresso into a bowl, and mix in the Kahlúa, if using. Dip half of the lady fingers into the espresso, and use them to line the bottom and sides of a 2½-quart serving bowl. Spread the Nutella mixture evenly in the bowl. Add the remaining lady fingers, dipped in the espresso. Cover with the mascarpone mixture. Refrigerate covered with plastic wrap until set, 4 to 5 hours, or overnight.

To serve, dust the tiramisù liberally with cocoa powder, and spoon it onto individual dessert plates.

ITALIAN CREPES WITH ESPRESSO SAUCE

If "manicotti" brings to mind those dried pasta tubes you see in the supermarket, then you would have found my mother's manicotti a revelation. Hers were luscious, meltingly soft crepes filled with ricotta cheese and swathed in homemade tomato sauce. This dessert is a sweet variation on that dish: It begins with my mother's manicotti crepe, fills it with a sweetened ricotta reminiscent of cannoli filling, and tops it with a creamy espresso sauce. For a more pronounced espresso flavor, skip the step of straining the sauce. SERVES 8

ESPRESSO SAUCE

1½ cups heavy cream

2½ tablespoons granulated sugar

1½ tablespoons ground espresso beans

Splash of rum, sambuca, or amaretto (whichever you use for the filling)

FILLING

1 tablespoon finely chopped raisins

1 tablespoon rum, sambuca, or amaretto

2 cups fresh whole-milk ricotta

¼ cup superfine or confectioners' sugar

2 teaspoons good-quality orange marmalade (large pieces minced)

½ teaspoon grated orange zest

2 tablespoons finely chopped semisweet chocolate

CREPES

1 cup all-purpose flour

Pinch of coarse salt

2 large eggs

1¾ cups milk

2 tablespoons canola oil

1 teaspoon grated orange zest

1 tablespoon granulated sugar

1 teaspoon vanilla extract

Unsalted butter

Confectioners' sugar

Prepare the sauce: Put the cream and sugar in a saucepan set over medium-high heat and bring to a boil, stirring to dissolve the sugar. Remove the pan from the heat and stir in the ground espresso beans. Cover and set aside for 20 minutes to infuse the cream with the flavor of the espresso. Strain through a fine-mesh sieve set over a bowl, and add the liqueur to the strained sauce. Refrigerate until cold, or up to 24 hours.

Make the filling: Combine the raisins and the rum in a small bowl, and set aside to steep for 20 minutes.

Place the fresh ricotta in a medium-size bowl and add the sugar, orange peel, orange zest, chocolate, and raisins. Cream together, using a spatula. Set aside. (The filling can be covered and refrigerated for up to 24 hours.)

Make the crepes: Pour the flour and salt into a medium-size bowl. Break the eggs into a separate bowl, and add the milk, canola oil, orange zest, sugar, and vanilla. Beat with a whisk until blended. Then gradually whisk the egg mixture into the flour until smooth and thoroughly incorporated.

Using a paper towel, lightly butter a small nonstick sauté pan. Set it over

medium-low heat. When the butter is hot but hasn't yet browned, add enough of the crepe batter to evenly coat the bottom. (If you pour too much batter into the pan, tilt the pan and pour the extra batter back into the bowl.) As soon as the surface looks set, after about 1 minute, use a metal spatula to help release the crepe, flip it, and cook on the other side for a few seconds. Transfer it to a platter and cover it loosely with a clean, slightly damp kitchen towel. Repeat with the rest of the batter, adjusting the heat to maintain a light golden color, and wiping the pan with butter between crepes when necessary to keep the pan greased and prevent the crepes from sticking. Keep the growing pile of crepes covered with the damp towel.

Place 2 to 3 tablespoons of the ricotta filling along the middle of each crepe, and roll the crepe up into a cylinder or wrap it like a small package.

The crepes can be prepared and filled in advance. Wrap them tightly in plastic wrap and refrigerate.

To serve, set 2 crepes in the center of each dessert plate, dust with confectioners' sugar, and garnish with a drizzle of the espresso sauce.

MIXED NUT BRITTLE

This glorified peanut brittle is made with cashews, slivered almonds, and pistachios, added to a freshly made caramel of butter and sugar. You can, of course, adapt the recipe to make your own house version by varying the assortment of nuts, or by choosing just one type. MAKES 3 POUNDS BRITTLE; SERVES 8 TO 10

2 cups salted cashews

2 cups salted pistachios

2 cups slivered almonds

6 cups sugar

12 tablespoons (1½ sticks) salted butter

Preheat the oven to 325°F.

Toast each type of nut separately by placing them in a single layer on a cookie sheet and baking until a little more than golden brown, 15 to 20 minutes for the cashews, 15 minutes for the pistachios, and 5 to 10 minutes for the almonds. As they are finished, let them cool to room temperature. Then gather them in a bowl and stir them together.

Put 2 cups of the sugar in a sauté pan and set it over medium-high heat. Let the sugar melt and caramelize until golden brown, approximately 4 minutes. Then add 4 tablespoons of the butter and whisk it with the sugar until it takes on an almost saucelike consistency. Remove the pan from the heat and stir in 2 cups of the nuts and stir until they are well coated in the caramel. Pour the mixture out onto a foil-lined baking sheet, spreading it out with a baking spatula. Repeat with the remaining sugar, butter, and nuts.

Put the baking sheets in the oven and bake until the nuts spread out into a flat sheet, approximately 10 minutes. Remove from the oven and let cool. Then break up by hand into desired-size pieces.

RUGALACH

This is a very traditional rugalach recipe. You can adapt it to make any number of variations by using a different jam in the apricot version or by changing the type of nuts in the chocolate rugalach. MAKES APPROXIMATELY 80 COOKIES

CREAM CHEESE DOUGH

8 ounces cold cream cheese

1 cup (2 sticks) cold unsalted butter, diced

1½ cups all-purpose flour

¼ cup plus 1 tablespoon sugar

1 cup walnuts

1 cup apricot jam

1 egg, beaten

1 cup sugar

8 ounces semisweet chocolate, finely grated on a box grater

1 cup (2 sticks) unsalted butter, cut up

Make the dough: Put all of the dough ingredients in the bowl of a standing mixer fitted with the paddle attachment, and paddle until thoroughly incorporated. If flour remains on the bottom of the bowl, turn the contents of the bowl out onto your work surface and knead the dough together by hand.

Wrap the dough in plastic wrap and flatten it to form a disk. Chill it in the refrigerator for 1 hour.

Unwrap the dough and roll it out on a lightly floured work surface to form six 14 by 4-inch rectangles that are ⅛ inch thick. Transfer the rectangles to sheets of parchment paper and refrigerate.

The dough can be made up to 1 week ahead of time, rolled between layers of parchment paper, wrapped well in plastic wrap, and frozen. Defrost before proceeding.

Make the cookies: Preheat the oven to 325°F.

Spread the nuts in a single layer on a baking sheet, and toast them in the oven until they are golden and fragrant, 10 to 15 minutes. Remove the pan from the oven and set aside to cool. Once the nuts are cool, finely chop them.

Put 1 dough rectangle on a sheet of parchment paper that is about 2 inches larger all around.

For the apricot rugalach: Spread ¼ cup of the jam over the dough, leaving a ⅛-inch border along the long sides of the rectangle. Use a pastry brush to spread a thin layer of egg along the exposed edges of dough.

Starting at a long side, roll the dough up to form a tight log, using the parchment paper to facilitate the rolling. Set the log on a baking sheet in the freezer.

Repeat with 2 more dough rectangles and the remaining filling, adding the logs to the baking sheet in the freezer. Freeze until frozen and hardened, or up to 1 week.

For the chocolate rugalach: Sprinkle 1 teaspoon of the sugar over the fourth rectangle, then top with 4 teaspoons of the grated chocolate and 2 tablespoons of the walnuts, leaving a ⅛-inch border along the long sides of the dough.

Starting at a long side, roll the dough up to form a tight log, using the parchment paper to facilitate the rolling. Set the log on a baking sheet in the freezer.

Repeat with the remaining 2 rectangles and filling, adding the logs to the baking sheet in the freezer.

Freeze until frozen and hardened, or for up to 1 week.

Preheat the oven to 325°F again.

Put the butter in a small saucepan and melt it over medium-low heat. Spread the remaining sugar out on your work surface.

Brush the outside of each rugalach log with melted butter, and roll it in the sugar to coat it.

Cut each log into eleven or twelve 1-inch pieces and set them, cut side up, on a parchment paper–lined cookie sheet, leaving 1 inch of space between them. Bake until golden brown, 8 to 10 minutes. Remove from the oven, let cool on a wire rack, and serve, or cover and store in an airtight plastic container at room temperature for up to 3 days.

COCONUT MACAROONS

My daughter, Victoria, an accomplished cook for her age, loves to bake these cookies. Although macaroons were originally made with egg whites, ground almonds, and sugar, she makes hers the way most Americans—myself included—do, emphasizing coconut over almonds. These macaroons are moist and chewy. Ideally they should be made with organic coconut, which is unsweetened and free of additives and has a purer flavor. It is readily available at health food stores. MAKES APPROXIMATELY 24 COOKIES

1 cup whole blanched almonds

3½ cups confectioners' sugar

1⅓ cups finely flaked, unsweetened organic coconut

4 extra-large egg whites

¼ teaspoon cream of tartar

A few tablespoons of your favorite jam, optional

Preheat the oven to 425°F. Line a cookie sheet with parchment paper.

Put the almonds in a food processor fitted with the steel blade and pulse just until they are crushed, taking care not to turn them to butter. Add the confectioners' sugar and coconut, and stir together until well integrated.

Fill a small saucepan with water and bring it to a low simmer over medium heat. Put the egg whites and cream of tartar in the bowl of a standing mixer. Hold the bowl over the simmering water and stir vigorously to take the chill off the egg whites and warm them slightly, but do not cook them. Return the bowl to the mixer, fit the mixer with the whip attachment, and whip the whites on medium-high speed until stiff peaks form.

Stir the coconut mixture into the egg whites. When they are combined, give the mixture a few extra strokes to deflate it a bit. This is your batter.

Fill a pastry bag fitted with a large round nozzle with the batter, and squeeze it to make rows of 1½-inch cookies, placing them about an inch apart, on the parchment-lined cookie sheet. Be sure to hold the bag upright, not at an angle. (You can also do this with a spoon if you don't have a pastry bag.) Place a second cookie sheet underneath the first (to prevent the cookies' bottoms from browning) and bake for 3 minutes. Lower the temperature to 375°F and continue baking until the macaroons' tops are golden, 12 to 15 minutes.

Slide the parchment paper, with the cookies on it, onto a wire rack to cool.

If any batter remains, cool the backs of the cookie sheet under cold running water, and repeat the baking process.

When the macaroons are cool, carefully peel them from the parchment paper. Gently sandwich two macaroons together. If desired, spoon ½ teaspoon of your favorite jam between the cookies before sandwiching them.

Store the macaroons in an airtight container for up to 1 week.

Note: If you prefer not to sandwich the macaroons, bake them without using the second cookie sheet.

INDEX